Søren Kierkegaard

Titles in the series Critical Lives present the work of leading cultural figures of the modern period. Each book explores the life of the artist, writer, philosopher or architect in question and relates it to their major works.

In the same series

# Søren Kierkegaard

Alastair Hannay

REAKTION BOOKS

Published by Reaktion Books Ltd
Unit 32, Waterside
44–48 Wharf Road
London N1 7UX, UK
www.reaktionbooks.co.uk

First published 2018

Printed and bound in Great Britain by Bell & Bain, Glasgow

A catalogue record for this book is available from the British Library

ISBN 978 1 78023 923 1

# Contents

# Preface

Many are familiar with the caricature of the man with the profiled nose, long upper-lip and receding chin, the stoop, top hat and stick, though sometimes umbrella. But our only real acquaintance with Søren Kierkegaard today is through his writings. How close, though, do we get to the human being in these? Much has been spoken and written on the mystery of the man behind the pseudonyms, as also on the disparity between their styles and that of the works signed with his own name. Who, then, was this unusual person with a name now becoming so familiar in so many contexts?

Literary theorists and theologians were the first to catch on to something new. But novelty was not at the front of Kierkegaard's mind, which was in no way radical in intention. Indeed he criticized his fellow citizens, and not least the clergy they listened to on Sundays, for ignoring perplexities and questions that not only Christians should be able to see and face. Yet he did so from an apparently unassailable belief in his own growing insight into the true nature of Christian faith. Some interpret this as of a piece with the historical contingency of a pietistic background and thus diminishing Kierkegaard's legacy. Others have glimpsed new insight into aspects of human nature not traditionally touched on by philosophy or even religion. Here was an unusual blend of radical and conservative that leaves these two options in an intriguing limbo, widely exploited, that has found adherents in not only literary theory but aesthetics, innovative ethics, theology, pedagogy, politics and the social order.

There are other uncertainties equally intriguing. At times Kierkegaard would speak of his own suffering in the light of the persecution of the early Christians. But he also admits that writing was an escape from personal torment. How much of the latter finds its way into the writing whether as topic (anxiety, despair) or as treatment (for instance an increasing appeal to a personal God)? Towards the end of his too-short life Kierkegaard confessed he could not represent in person the Christianity presented by his latest pseudonym. In asking it of others and himself he had been, after all, 'only a poet'.

Subjectivity, inwardness and the single individual are the notions that surface most clearly throughout the authorship. Far from some state of mind hidden from the biographer's or historian's view, what is translated 'inwardness' (*Inderlighed*) is concerted action in the light of some 'idea' or living vision whose reference is the world we share. By action being concerted we usually mean an action carried out by several people, but for Kierkegaard it can be said that an individual's action is concerted when focused by an idea or ideal that brings conflicting drives and considerations together in the engagement of a unified self. By his own engagement with the world, polemically and provocatively, in the spirit of this conception and on its behalf, Kierkegaard made himself a social outsider. But it was a role for which he seems to have been well suited as well as destined.

Some claim that, to the discerning reader, there is a personal signature to all of Kierkegaard's writings, whether signed or pseudonymous, and that it becomes evident once the variety of genres and diversity of topics come into collective focus under the rubric of Kierkegaard's critical (as one might say) 'un'-settlement with his own society. That, as much else, must be left to the reader's judgement. But with someone whose life was so closely linked to his writing, it helps to look critically at the life. It can be viewed from both ends: prospectively we can ask how a wealthy family's spoilt child and inattentive and impudent schoolboy could become the author of a series of curiously innovative and strangely disturbing books, and retrospectively we can ask in what way and how far Kierkegaard's preoccupation with his themes still bears on our own cultural situation. If Kierkegaard wrote to keep his demons at bay, he also wrote about how he came by them, indeed so wholeheartedly that his exertions were a factor in his early death. It is hardly irrelevant that what captured his attention was not life as seen by the social observer but as it is revealed to one with unusual powers of self-observation. Not least was it due to an ability to put words to questions seldom asked or even formulated or which, if asked, are typically given facile answers.

If the works can indeed speak to us today, and perhaps to some they do so more compellingly than they did to his contemporaries, this can in part be due to the lasting influence of his own writings, but also to that of other writers who stood similarly outside their own societies. The stance of the outsider is and has been all too easily romanticized. In Kierkegaard's case, except when his poetic imagination overdramatized a martyr role that had gripped him from his earliest student years, his part in the role of 'exception' is open-eyed and unsentimental. He looks long, and in the end dispassionately, at the facts of a life led outside the 'universals' in which we count ourselves as for better or worse belonging; and he confronts the reader with the subversive idea that the exception's vantage-point is that from which true belonging is not only best seen but also best brought about. However outrageous, the wit, imagination and humour with which Kierkegaard offers this proposal has found him followers in social aliens as far afield, and apart, as Woody Allen and Franz Kafka.

Luplau Janssen, *Søren Kierkegaard* (1813–1855), 1902.

# 1

# Rags to Riches

Behind the question of how a rich man's son came to be the world-famous author, there lurks another: how did the father, born to a poor peasant family and in formal bondage, become one of Denmark's wealthiest men? Michael Pedersen Kierkegaard was born as one of nine on 12 December 1756 on a farm on the windswept lowland of western Jutland. The farm was called 'Østre Kirkegaard' (East Churchland). (The first 'e' in his own name was later supplied by Michael Pedersen himself.) The 'Kirkegaard' cognomen identified the Pedersens as working custodians of church-owned land, which naturally enough included the graveyard. In urban surroundings, the name would mean simply 'graveyard' or 'cemetery'. Customarily, the land was worked to support the parish priest, but Sæding parish was too poor to support a priest of its own, and the 'glebe', as such areas are traditionally known, had been rented to Michael Pedersen's family. The church had been built in the twelfth century in Romanesque style, and was, in its way, the only civic centre. Without a spire pointing to any particular part of the vast Jutland sky, the whole firmament could point down instead at the congregation, directing its thoughts to the divine protector above. In doing so, it would also remind them of what was owed if they were to deserve better in this life or the next.

Sæding is still an area of scattered dwellings and hamlets. It lies 14.5 km (9 miles) east of Ringkøbing Fjord, an inland lake protected from the sea by a long coastal strip through which a narrow strait allows North Sea fishermen access to a safe haven. Except to shepherds, peat-diggers and a priest or two, the area had little to offer in the way of livelihoods. Nor was it easy for those born there to move elsewhere. Farmhands were subject to a form of 'homestead' bondage (*Stavnsbåndet*) that – in periods of their maturity, of varying length through the years of its enforcement – forbade peasant males (*Bondekarle*) from leaving their places of work. The law was intended to ensure a supply of able-bodied sailors or soldiers in time of war, and failure to comply meant a hefty fine. In 1788 the law was relaxed and in 1800 finally repealed. By then Michael Pedersen was 34 years old and doing well in Copenhagen.

Although the free movement of farmhands inside their particular area was also restricted by law, it was allowed by agreement between landowners. As a young boy, Michael Pedersen had been taken on by a farming and sheep-dealing cousin of his father. Aware of the boy's intelligence, the cousin took him at the age of eleven to an uncle, Niels Andersen Sædding, by then a prospering textile trader in Copenhagen. Wool and Jutland being synonymous, the cloth trade was a natural conduit for the importation of business skills from that part of Denmark. At the age of 21, Michael Pedersen Kierkegaard, industrious and astute and with a career as errand boy and shop assistant behind him, was officially released from 'bondage' by the home priest in a document allowing him 'free pass, to be and to live where he will without begging my permission in the future'.

On receiving his citizen's rights, Michael Pedersen went into business himself and did well, first as a travelling clothier in Danish woollens, and then as a wholesale importer of cloth and textiles with a royal patent to

> deal in East Indian and Chinese goods, as well as goods from our West Indian islands such as sugar (refined and unrefined), syrup

and coffee beans . . . and to sell same as wholesale or retail to all and sundry.[1]

Through industry, good management and lucky investments, the former shepherd boy became hosier Kierkegaard, and at the age of 29, together with a friend, he had earned enough to buy a house in the suburban town of Hillerød. In 1794 he married Kirstine Nielsdatter Røyen, the sister of a business partner. When, two years later, his benefactor uncle died, Michael Pedersen inherited his estate.

In that same year, 1796, his wife too died of pneumonia and childless. She had a maid, Ane Sørensdatter Lund, a distant cousin of Michael's who had been offered this job in town. Shortly after Kirstine's death, Ane became pregnant, and Michael Pedersen, making what he must have thought was the best of a bad job, offered her a mean-minded marriage contract: it appears they had not been in any sense lovers, the pregnancy doubtless due to an unguarded moment of shared loneliness. In the prenuptial arrangement drafted by Michael Pedersen, Ane was denied the usual inheritance and became virtually his employee with a salary and fixed annual housekeeping budget. There was no provision for her in the event of divorce, not even custody of the child. The officials registering the contract were aghast but could do nothing. The couple married on 26 April 1797, and a daughter baptized Maren Kirstine was born just over four months later on 7 September. It was at this juncture that the now forty-year-old Michael decided to put his prosperous business into the hands of trustees and to live in retirement.

Among the several possible reasons for Michael's decision was his state of health; he felt unwell and thought he might be on the point of dying. But there were longer-term reasons. His income as a rentier was enough to maintain his family without his continued business involvement, and he did not trust Ane with the day-to-day housekeeping. By staying at home, he might also avoid public shame at the hasty marriage with a young servant girl who was also a cousin; as a deeply religious man, he would have felt the need both to nurture and atone for his private transgression.

At the back of his mind, however, there may have been an allegedly definitive experience from the Jutland heath that has become an enduring legacy in the Kierkegaard lore. It seems unlikely, however, that it troubled him at the time as much as it would do in his old age following the several tragedies he was to endure. As his youngest son-to-be was to note many years later in his journal,

> How dreadful the thought of that man who once, as a small boy tending sheep on the Jutland heath, in much suffering, starving and exhausted, stood up on a hill and cursed God – and that man was unable to forget it when he was 82 years old.[2]

At that time, however, Michael Pedersen had to think of his family's future. If, as was likely in those days, there were to be more children, and in particular boys, Ane was not to be entrusted with their upbringing. Michael Pedersen Kierkegaard did not die; he lived to be 82, and there were to be more children aplenty. Against all expectation, the marriage proved to be a success. It ended 37 years later with Ane's death in July 1834.

Within the next eight years, there were two more daughters, Nicoline Christine and Petrea Severine, followed by the eldest son Peter Christian. After the family had moved to a house in Copenhagen, a son, Søren Michael, was born, in 1807. Another move was to a large house on Nytorv (New Market) next to the Court House. It became their established home. Another son, Niels Andreas, was born there in 1809. Four years later, on 5 May 1813, when his father was 57, almost as an afterthought, came Søren Aabye.

Søren was to speak of himself as having been born in the 'wrong' fiscal year in which 'so many other bad banknotes were put into circulation'.[3] The force of 'other' will detain us later, but the circumstances are worth recording. The future self-professed bad penny was only six years old when his brother Søren Michael, known as Michael, died at the age of twelve of a brain haemorrhage following an accident in the school playground. Michael had been born in March 1807; in August of that year, the British fleet bombarded Copenhagen. This was the second time the British had attacked the Danish capital. The first had been in 1801 when the 43-year-old warrior seaman Horatio Nelson, under the command of Sir Hyde Parker, nineteen years older than Nelson, famously put his telescope to his blind eye and was 'damned' if he could see the signal commanding him to withdraw. At that time, the threat to Great Britain had been a neutrality pact that Russia had initiated in 1800 with Denmark in an attempt to forge stronger ties with Napoleon. For the British, it would mean losing the Baltic States as supply sources for the Royal Navy. On this second occasion, in

In 1808 Michael Pedersen Kierkegaard established the family home on Nytorv, here depicted in 1839.

1807, the threat was again to the sea lanes in the North Sea and Baltic. Although ostensibly neutral, Denmark was being pressed by France as well as Russia to give Napoleon the benefit of its fleet. The city suffered considerable damage from rocket-fired missiles personally supervised by their inventor William Congreve, one of them removing the spire of Vor Frue Kirke (the Church of Our Lady). The entire Danish fleet having been commandeered, a period of economic decline began which led to state bankruptcy in that 'wrong' year of 1813.

Although it was a bad fiscal year for many, prescient or lucky as usual, Michael Pedersen had just before the crash bought guaranteed gold-convertible bonds and came out of it, if anything, even better off.[4] As the children reached the appropriate age, he began attending assiduously to their religious guidance. Pastor Bull at the church of the Holy Spirit seemed a suitably intelligent and sincere representative of the Lutheran Church who could give the children a solid start in the state church. Michael Pedersen's personal leanings were to the Congregation of Moravian Brothers or Herrnhuters. With its hold among the peasant community, he would have known of the Brotherhood from his childhood. The Moravians had, as early as 1727, sent emissaries to Denmark, and their growing influence was such that by the time Michael Pedersen was prospering in Copenhagen, the brethren had founded, on what had been bare land, the town of Christianfeld in southern Jutland. The Brotherhood's own centre was in Herrnhut (literally, 'the Lord's keeping') in Saxony, but the real centre of a Moravian's life was God and the local church. With a teaching almost diametrically opposed to that of the liberal-rationalist Lutheranism prevailing at the time in Denmark, Moravians spoke to the feelings rather than to the intellect. The movement was anticlerical and preached inner rebirth, while its egalitarianism made it indifferent to the outer trappings of bourgeois life. In Copenhagen, the Congregation of Moravian Brothers had grown significantly with the destruction

Kierkegaard caricature from a recent scholarly publication.

and widespread bankruptcy following the Napoleonic Wars. Hosier Kierkegaard's business had miraculously escaped, and when, in 1816, the Moravians decided that their meeting house in Copenhagen was too small, he was chosen as chairman of the building committee for a new house on Stormgade, a short walk from the Kierkegaard home and large enough to seat six hundred brothers. Michael Pedersen's benefactions did not stop there; he also made gifts to the church in Sæding and financed a new house there for his mother and two sisters.

Conscious of his new social position, Michael Pedersen's beginnings made him seek ways of consolidating it. In 1812 a young, erudite and concerned Lutheran preacher by the name of Mynster had appeared on the scene. In him, Michael Pedersen saw a useful compromise. Later to become primate of the state church, Jakob Peter Mynster started his career in heated opposition to the intellectualism of the Lutheran establishment, with its university base, and also to the Enlightenment rationalism that rejected many long-standing tenets of Christian faith, including revelation. He came to Copenhagen from a parish in southern Zealand, where he had been plagued by doubts about the faith he was proclaiming to his peasant congregation. Preaching the Gospel as though it were history when, for him, it had 'almost an exclusive poetic value' was a personal trial that threw him into despair. A resulting crisis seems, however, to have resolved itself happily. Mynster said later that he had 'to feel [him]self utterly and painfully abandoned in the world in order to find what is the highest and most blessed of all'.[5] Whatever it was that confirmed him in his discovery, Mynster's new sense of conviction served him well and would propel him to the top of his calling. This proved to be a blessing for the state church too, since Mynster's sense of the need for a form of devotion that was personal catered nicely to the emotional needs of the growing numbers of those who were becoming disenchanted with the aridly intellectual character of the state church. Kierkegaard senior was not slow to see the combined personal and social advantages of a family affiliation with a preacher who, like the Moravians, appealed to the living sense of God but fell short of the anticlericalism which, if it spread, could leave the state church without a following. By the time the little Søren began attending church, it was Mynster's sermons that the family were taken to hear on Sunday mornings. And it was by Pastor Mynster that Søren would be confirmed in the Church of Our Lady on 20 April 1828. In the evenings, they still attended the Congregation of Brothers, however.

On weekdays during the school term, a fair proportion of the children (those at least five years old) were out of the house from before nine in the morning until seven in the evening, though free on Saturday afternoons. With the time now at his disposal during the day, Michael Pedersen could devote himself to his own neglected education. An autodidact with a taste for philosophy and a talent for argument, Kierkegaard senior was especially interested in the early eighteenth-century German rationalist and Leibnizian Christian Wolff (1679–1754). The former shepherd boy with no education preferred reading *Vernunftige Gedanken von Gott, der Welt und der Seele der Menschen, auch allen Dingen überhaupt* (Reflections on God, the World, the Soul of Man, and Things in General, 1720) in German. But when they were at home, he could also take time off to entertain his sons with his rich imagination, though it seems only Søren was temperamentally disposed to gratify his father in this respect. Niels Andreas, who is said to be the one who most resembled the mother, was less willing to fall in with his father's schemes. Peter Christian, it seems, was too self-important to be very imaginative.

According to Søren, it was his own father who gave him insight into the nature of 'God's fatherly love'. Writing later of God's 'unchangeableness', he also noted that he had never known his father other than as unchangeably 'old'.[6] Putting such onus on a father known only as an old man would prove a risky psychological investment. When Michael Pedersen was to tell his sons of the sins of his youth – and not only as a young boy cursing God on that heath – they were devastated. As for the heath, after his father's death and on his sole visit to Sæding, Søren was to write,

The heath must be peculiarly suited to developing spiritual strength; here everything lies *naked* and *unveiled* before God, and there is no place here for all those distractions, the many nooks and crannies in which consciousness can take cover and from which seriousness often has difficulty catching up with *distracted* thoughts. Here consciousness has to take a firm and

Kierkegaard's father, Michael Pedersen Kierkegaard (1756–1838).

precise grip on itself. 'Whither shall I flee from thy presence?' is something one can truly say on the heath.[7]

In practice, the home provided by Michael Pedersen for his family was a domestic version of that same heath. Not a vast landscape under the tyranny of an oppressive sky, it was an enclosure from which there was still no fleeing from God's presence. Just as a twelve-year-old Michael Pedersen could not deny God but only curse him, so could a 41-year-old Søren note in his journal that a sense of being ignored by God was the 'most fearful of all [of God's] punishments'.[8] God's absence could never signify his non-existence.

Kierkegaard's mother, Ane Sørensdatter Lund Kierkegaard (1768–1834).

Yet nothing indicates that the Kierkegaard home was a fundamentally unhappy one. A fellow pupil whom Søren took home was 'attracted by the odd, old hosier and the serious, sombre, but loving tone which characterized the relationship between him and his sons'. Michael Pedersen said he suffered from insomnia and told the fourteen-year-old visitor, 'When I can't sleep, I lie down and talk with my boys, and there are no better conversations here in Copenhagen.'[9] Of the mother, we hear almost nothing; these conversations were well above her head. However, a relative who as a child knew the family describes her as 'the mild, gentle sunbeam of [Søren's] childhood home'.

A granddaughter recalled 'a kind little woman with an unpretentious and cheerful turn of mind'. Her

> plump little figure was only to appear in the doorway of the nursery and the cries and screams would give way to a hush; the rebellious young boy or girl soon fell sweetly asleep in her soft embrace.[10]

Søren is said even as an early teenager to have clung continually to his mother's apron strings, but for reasons worth speculating on, the 21-year-old Søren makes no mention even of her death, although someone who knew him well at that time said, 'never in her life had she seen a human being so deeply distressed as S. Kierkegaard by the death of his mother'.[11]

It was nevertheless Michael Pedersen Kierkegaard's guilt-prone personality that overshadowed the indisputable love that he himself showed to his children. Whatever the true source of the guilt, the death at the age of 24 of his favourite daughter, Maren Kirstine, a year after Søren began school, must have torn his soul as well as pierced his heart. She had been conceived out of wedlock. Whatever the causes or connections, the result of Michael Pedersen Kierkegaard's oppressively theocratic regime would be the mental collapse in old age of one son, the death in obscurity of another and the local notoriety and quite unanticipated worldwide fame of a third.

## 2

# The Bad Penny

Peter Christian had been a prize pupil at the School of Civic Virtue when Søren began there in 1822, and he was constantly reminded of his elder brother's prowess. A testimonial provided by the headmaster when Søren left school nine years later, in typical fashion included the remark,

> once his fine intellectual abilities are able to develop more freely and unconstrainedly at the university, he will certainly be among the more capable students and in many ways will come to resemble his oldest brother.[1]

There are many recorded memories of Kierkegaard's schooldays. Their reliability is lessened by the fact that they were provided on demand after Kierkegaard's death and may reflect attitudes towards his later celebrity, but a fairly vivid portrait may nevertheless be extracted from these recollections. The image they present is conflicted: a combination of cheeky brat, whose 'foul mouth' cost him many a 'bloody nose', and a loner who never spoke of home.[2] Although the headmaster's testimonial also recorded a 'good mind, receptive to everything that requires special application', its possessor is said 'for a long time' to have been 'exceedingly childish and quite devoid of seriousness'.[3] Less disliked than feared by his school pupils, Søren could still be remembered with fondness. One of them recalled a 'quaintly dressed fellow, slight, small for his age, pale and freckled'. With no experience of the closed society of a boys' school, old hosier Kierkegaard had outfitted his son in a way that more or less invited fellow pupils to call him 'choirboy'. His father's trade also led to a nickname, 'Søren Sock'.[4] Søren did only moderately well in class – usually coming second or third – seemingly without doing much homework, however, and he was accused in one report of using a crib sheet under his desk.[5] One teacher scolded him for plagiarizing a sermon by Mynster, the family priest, which at least bears testimony to his father's devoted care of the son's soul. The same teacher said that what annoyed him about young Kierkegaard most was that he had an answer ready even before receiving the question. Some teachers thought he 'lacked diligence' and treated them with 'impudence'.

On one occasion, his fellow pupils bound and beat him because they resented his 'all-conquering dialectic', although that expression may again reflect a later time. That particular occasion, however, says much: another ex-pupil said it had been dangerous to quarrel with Søren, because he 'knew how to make his opponent appear ridiculous'. It is hard to doubt altogether the claim that when Peter Christian came to teach Søren's class, his younger brother used the situation deliberately to make fun of him.[6]

'Dialectic' is from *dialektikos*, the Greek word for the art of discussion and argument. Its use in arriving at truths, including in revealing ignorance, is first brought to light in Plato's Socratic dialogues. In the philosophical world that was to be Kierkegaard's intellectual forum, 'dialectic' meant a developing interchange between incompatible thoughts aimed – or as in Hegel, aiming itself – at an ultimate resolution. For Hegel, this, the Absolute, was where consciousness becomes conscious of itself as all reality. In a way, Kierkegaard can be classified along with Marx as a dialectical thinker directly opposed to what both regarded as such abstract thought-spinning. For both, reality as we are forced to live it reveals itself most cogently and truthfully in the form of the need to resolve oppositions from which we try to look away, and their resolutions have to be achieved by decisive action. For Marx, the tensions are found in the working arrangements of society, the corresponding resolutions requiring political action on the part of those collectives best placed to grasp the situation and resolve them, if necessary by revolution. The tensions that Kierkegaard brings to mind concern dilemmas faced by individuals in their personal confrontation with life independently of political and economic variables. Now, at this very early stage in his life, he was being exposed to living exponents of that venerable adversarial art of conversation known as debate.

Søren and Peter Christian took different lessons from their father's demonstrations of his taste and talent for debate. Where Peter Christian adapted himself to his father's debating style in a way that made it a profession, Søren was to use the same demonstrations to cast doubt on the pretensions of thought itself. When Peter Christian came home from Germany in September 1830 with a doctorate from Göttingen, his notable skills as a speaker had earned him the title of 'devil debater from the North' (*Der Disputierteufel aus dem Norden*). But when it comes to devils, it is worth quoting the Faroese writer William Heinesen, in whose novel *The Doomed Fiddlers* Søren Kierkegaard is described as 'going one better'. Unrivalled in the art of 'attacking reason with its own weapons', Kierkegaard turned them not only against others but in the end 'against himself' and 'like that devil *chargé d'affaires* in Goethe's *Faust*', he was the possessor of a superior intellect 'which he deploys with the same supple facility and tirelessness'. Kierkegaard was not 'just Mephistopheles but at the same time Mephistopheles's victim, man, Faust'.[7]

Turning his weapons against others was to become Søren Kierkegaard's forte but was a pattern discernible from the start. His schoolmates say that his stabs came unexpectedly and 'usually directed at big, tall, and strongly built boys'. Whether by choice or compulsion, the small, thin Søren 'pounced upon tall fellows who were intellectual midgets'.[8] But many have experienced how, in school, oddity must assert itself or go under. Though used in the first instance as protection, the appearance to others can often be one of superiority and self-assertion. Even when there is something worth attacking, instead of taking it on in its own terms, the weapon of reason may be used simply to pick holes in the opposing view. This, as often as not, is just another way of getting one's own back on the person advancing the view, not an attack on the view itself. It is a weapon that can be used not only to bring down intellectual midgets with impressive physiques, but intellectual giants with undeveloped souls.

Part of the rivalry between Peter Christian and Søren would be their contrasting attitudes to Nicolai Frederik Severin Grundtvig, a theologian, politician, pastor, educationist, historian, philologist and eventually one of Scandinavia's greatest educational influences. When Peter Christian was studying at the university in the early 1820s, there was already a group of brilliant young Grundtvigian theologians, some of whom would become Søren's friends. They spoke to the living faith of his father but, unlike the Moravians, in a style conveniently suited to an aspiring professor rather than the son of a peasant. As an alternative father figure, Grundtvig offered the intellectually aspiring Peter Christian an escape from his claustrophobically theocratic home. Søren, on the other hand, with his actual father the image in which he saw God, openly despised Grundtvig. He sided with his father's pastor against his brother's new mentor. How much of Kierkegaard's later lampooning of Grundtvig as an intellectual midget in the guise of a giant is sincere is uncertain. Certainly the exuberant atmosphere that Grundtvigianism exuded (that 'little troupe of enthusiasts who are trained in Pastor Grundtvig's ale-Norse tavern'[9]) was totally alien to his own temperament; and yet there is much in Grundtvig that Kierkegaard seems also to have admired. *His* soul was certainly not undeveloped, and Grundtvig had a spontaneity that Søren, of whom

The theologian, historian, poet and educationist N.F.S. Grundtvig (1783–1872), by P. C. Skovgaard, 1847.

someone later said that he 'seemed to live only as a thought', must have envied.[10] The scorn he records in his journal did not prevent Søren from polite exchanges with Grundtvig on the street.

For all his diligence and the respect he received from teachers and students, Peter doubtless suffered more than his younger brother. He was exposed to the paternal regime longer and, as the eldest son, was both expected and required to deliver more. His diligence and success were an undisputed fact, as was Michael Pedersen Kierkegaard's undoubted pleasure in them. But he was also under pressure, while Søren seems to have been in the happy situation of being able to count on his father's support whatever he did, or didn't; even failure to show progress in theology was indulged. It would be surprising if Peter did not feel the rivalry as much as Søren. Apart from the preferential treatment, Peter actively disliked him for not respecting his own dutiful behaviour and sense of family honour. Peter's puzzlement, and the piquant situation in the family, are captured by a letter that their father wrote to Peter Christian while he was in Germany.

> I do not know what the matter is with Søren. I cannot make him write to you. I wonder whether it is intellectual poverty that prevents him thinking of something to write about or childish vanity that keeps him from writing anything except what he will be praised for, and, in so far as he is unsure about it in this case, whether that is why he won't write anything.

Søren, given the task of transcribing this letter in the copybook that his father kept of his correspondence, took the opportunity to add in the letter itself, 'I (Søren) will soon write to you so that I may be able also to gainsay Father.'[11] The implication that Peter Christian's complaint was already gainsaid by the addition is typical of the sharp-minded little mischief-maker.

Aside from the unpredictable bouts of teasing, at school it is said that Søren was a 'silent and unspeaking existence' and except for that one fellow pupil who gained a sense of the mood at the hosier's home, Michael Pedersen remained 'shrouded in mysterious shadows of strictness and eccentricity'.[12] Was his home a holy of holies or a place where Søren could hang his protective wit on the coat stand by the door? It was not, it seems, the latter, for Søren was known for exercising his wit there too, and not always to the amusement of his family. The habit even earned him the pet name 'the Fork'. According to a sister's reported account, it originated at a dinner when, on being asked what he wanted to be, Søren replied, 'A fork.' When asked why, he had said, 'Then I could spear anything I wanted on the dinner table.' When further asked, 'what if we came after you?' the reply was, 'Then I'll spear you.'[13]

Peter Christian, after returning from his travels in Germany in 1830 with a doctoral thesis in Latin (with the translated title 'On the Concept and Wickedness of Lying') duly defended, showed no signs of getting married or moving out. The two married sisters having left some years earlier, the next departure would be that of brother Niels Andreas in 1832. Niels, preferring books and learning and with no desire to accede to his father's wish that he continue the family's trading tradition, had squabbled for some time with his father over his future. Peter was, of course, excused, since he was to establish the family's intellectual respectability. As for Søren, whatever his future might be, there was no indication that he could look after money; indeed, his forte would prove to be using it. Niels Andreas left for the United States to make his mark in the New World, but, following a year of disappointments, he died less than a year later of tuberculosis in Paterson, New Jersey, at just 24 years old. Ironically, with his surname, he was the first to be buried in a newly consecrated burial ground. At home, this event further worsened a mood already dampened by the death in the previous year of 33-year-old Nicoline following childbirth. Nor did it help that Niels Andreas had asked on his deathbed to be remembered to his mother but made no mention of his father. The litany of loss was to continue. In the following July, Ane, Michael Pedersen's wife of 38 years, died, and at the end of the same year, so did his last remaining daughter, Petrea Severine, as her sister had, after childbirth.

Depressions have many causes and seldom have clear focuses on what they are about. In this, they are like the state of mind that Kierkegaard would elaborate in *The Concept of Anxiety* some years later, saying that anxiety 'differs altogether from fear and similar concepts that refer to something definite'.[14] What the actual causes were in this case can only be conjectured, but there are obvious candidates. The father's morbidity has often been cited – under one roof, depressions can become infectious. Strangely enough, the death of the mother is no more mentioned in this context than was her actual living existence. We might surmise, however, that for Søren, it swept from beneath him a safety net that in the nature of his busy mind would be difficult for him to express, even if he did reflect on it; his relationship with his mother would not be the kind of thing the witty youth was used to putting to words. There has been speculation over what an entry in his journals from 1843 refers to when it says that after his own death, no one would find the least information in his papers about what had 'really' filled his life.[15] He called this a 'consolation'; it was the 'script' in his 'innermost being' that 'explains everything' and when taken away, turned important things, even for him, into trifles. Whether or not the script was so internal as to defy articulation and was consequently only metaphorically a script, the removal of a backcloth of motherly care can surely have been at least part of what caused the youngest son's depression.

Another cause could be the woodenly religious Peter Christian. Always within the confines of religion, if one may so put it, but at times teetering at its edge, Søren had a lifelong ambivalence towards Christianity. He could look at his father's faith dispassionately and describe the dread associated in his mind with Christianity as due to his father's ministrations; but he could also talk of what he 'suffered on account of Peter when . . . morbidly seized by the religious'.[16] Peter Christian's relation to cultural Christianity was morbid because it was immediate: not merely unquestionable, it was simply not questioned. His life depended on it, and when it failed, he had to make religious penance. Peter Christian also suffered bouts of depression, but the younger brother appears in his reflective mind to have had the means to protect himself from the worst effects of living under their shared roof. Could it have been because of Søren's ability, or was it his compulsion, to put *everything* 'into reflection'? This was what he later claimed to do regarding Christianity: 'casting [it] and becoming a Christian wholly and fully into reflection.'[17] But that too could be a source of depression. Some things resist reflection, and putting 'everything' into reflection either leaves the reflecting *person* still to be sized up and – with its wordless worries – unaccounted for, or else, by supposedly including the person *in* the reflection (he 'seemed to live only as a thought'), it leaves nothing for the reflecting person actually to be.

# 3

# Audience

The earliest papers, which date from Kierkegaard's first university years (1831–2), are mainly in the form of notes, transcriptions and translations. There are theological notes dating from December 1833 and March 1834, some of them taking up Schleiermacher's notion of religious experience as being based on a feeling of absolute dependence (does prayer then become a 'fiction'?).[1] Friedrich Schleiermacher, chief theological spokesman of the Romantic movement and close friend of its literary prophet Friedrich Schlegel, himself atheist turned Catholic, located religion in a specific state of mind. Although the notion of a quality of 'inwardness' introduced in the pseudonymous works is easily mistaken for a revision of that notion, religiousness in Kierkegaard's writings becomes a matter of personal will and action with a clear notion of the distance between God and believer, while prayer becomes a way of changing the one who prays, not an attempt to bend the will of an unchangeable God.[2]

The journals, starting in April 1834, are not diaries; they remain silent about things at home, his mother's death or his brother's typhus. It is only from Peter Christian's conventional daily journal that we learn why, on the Friday before Easter week in 1834, Søren attended communion with his father and mother but without Peter Christian: the two sons were not on speaking terms. Nor does Kierkegaard comment on his university studies – not, for instance, on the fact that they should be finishing by now. The only available comments in this respect are in a draft letter addressed to a palaeontologist brother-in-law in Brazil, dated 1 June 1835: 'I am embarked on studies for the theological examination, a pursuit which does not interest me in the least and which therefore is not going particularly quickly.'[3] This explains some of the role that Kierkegaard's journals came to play and also their content: they chart and develop the *disjecta membra* of an unfocused period of study with a view to bringing them into some as-yet-unidentified perspective. That the focus would be on matters beyond the boundaries of their traditional hub, academic theology, would make any unifying effort even less clear. The journals could also record provisional conclusions, as in an entry from 17 October 1835 stating that 'philosophy and Christianity can never be united.'[4] At the time, any philosophy without reference to theology was practically unthinkable, but in Kierkegaard's mind, if Christianity were to continue to be a part of the dialectic, it would have to be in some form other than that favoured by liberal-minded rationalists, who seemed to find it so easy to situate it in their own unifying perspective.

In Kierkegaard lore, the Gilleleje Testament, dated 1 August 1835 – along with the young Michael Pedersen's cursing God on the Jutland heath and Kierkegaard's later self-confessed 'thorn in the flesh' – is one of the images regularly relied upon for homing in on Kierkegaard's thought and life. The most often-quoted statement by Kierkegaard says,

> What I really need is to be clear about *what I am to do*, not what I must know, except in the way knowledge must precede all action. It is a question of understanding my own destiny, of seeing what the Deity really wants *me* to do; the thing is to find a truth which is truth *for me*, to find *the idea for which I am willing to live and die*.

He adds,

> What use would it be in this respect if I were to discover a
> so-called objective truth, or if I worked my way through the
> philosophers' systems and were able to call them all to account
> on request, point out inconsistencies in every single circle?[5]

Pointing out inconsistencies in each other's thinking was the way
philosophers worked in practice, and Søren, as one would expect
and to which many journal entries testify, was superlative in this
area. But what could such an *idea* be for which he would be willing
to live and die? And why was it so crucial?

It is unlikely that this idea could 'fill his life' in the way of the
hidden 'script', which explained everything, in his 'innermost
being'. An idea can be scripted quite openly, as an aim for instance,
or in Sartrean terms, a 'basic project'. You may keep it to yourself,
but if you do anything about it in practice, even if only as a writer, it
comes somehow into the open. It seems more likely that the longing
for an idea that would give meaning to Kierkegaard's life was in
some way *due* to that hidden script, itself a negative state of mind,
one of loss, and which left him looking at the world, life itself, his
own life and existence as a whole as an empty space to be filled with
something. Filling it would require an ideal which was his to decide
upon, since no one in possession of any merely 'objective' truth
was in a position to supply him with anything 'bound up with the
deepest roots of [his] existence'. To find that 'idea' would be 'more
properly to find [him]self'. His five years at the university had been
a period of accumulation that merely expanded his horizons. He
was like 'a man who had collected furniture and rented rooms but
still hasn't found the beloved with whom to share life's ups and
downs'.[6]

The remark foreshadows a future when that beloved would be
found without any realistic prospect of such sharing. Yet, by looking
back, it also contains hints at what the writings that followed that
fateful discovery would contain. 'Vainly,' writes Kierkegaard,

I have sought an anchorage, not just in the depths of knowledge but in the bottomless sea of pleasure. I have felt the well-nigh irresistible power with which one pleasure holds out its hand to another – I have also felt the tedium, the laceration, which ensues.[7]

Finding not everything suited to his mind, he 'withdrew with an awareness of [his] own competence, rather as a worn-out clergyman resigns with his pension', but had failed to find his 'I'. Learning to know one's self must come before properly knowing anything else: 'Only when the person has inwardly understood himself and then sees the course forward from the path he is to take' does his life acquire 'repose and meaning'. This 'I' is not to be found in 'the sphere of knowledge', for there we are told by philosophers to begin with a Socratic 'not-knowing' – that is to say, with nothing. Worse still is being told to begin with ethical correctness – 'the navigable waters of morality [*Sædelighedens Farvande*]'. Those 'who have yet to enter the trade winds of virtue' are 'tossed about in the most terrible way . . . feel[ing] happy and content one moment in a resolve to go down the right path, only to hurl [themselves] into the abyss of despair the next'. Something more stable was called for. Kierkegaard refers to the Kingdom of Heaven, it being the search for and discovery of this that was 'the first thing to be resolved'. The Deity is still and everlastingly, as well as unchangingly, in place. A note from a few days previously talks of an Archimedean point 'outside the confines of time and space'.[8] It is in its (in Kierkegaard's eyes very close) relation to this that the 'I' takes its own stand and takes responsibility, but also by analogy finds in itself the satisfaction that a good theory in natural science gives to its discoverer 'peace, harmony and joy'.[9]

Kierkegaard reveals here what might seem an unexpected aspect of his wandering studies: a keen interest in science. A heavenly body's nature is not decided by how it looks, or by how it is related to other heavenly bodies; these 'externals' are consequences of 'the harmony of centrifugal and centripetal forces that bring it into being, the rest being left 'to develop by itself'.[10] So too with us: the 'I' we cannot find in thought or action is established outside it all in some way prior to all that we can discover or decide in thought or action.

Once started, the themes of pleasure and ethics, and a God that we can relate to only by rising above the 'externals' of our identities in time, will become the twine whose strands unwind in the authorship. They would be unwound and rewound in terms of a concept of a life-view, a unifying principle that is imposed on life and not imparted by life. A life-view would provide a key to understanding further details within its own frame, although it would also throw light on the past. Just now, however, Kierkegaard is in the throes of his own past, a disorganized past, a past of wide reading, random teahouse chat and eager talking with fellow students down the streets of Copenhagen. Rather than anticipating the future, he is putting himself on what he believed would be the right path forward, though accurately predicting the struggle it would entail:

> I am crossing the Rubicon! This road no doubt leads me into *battle*, but I will not give up. I will not lament the past – why lament? I will work with vigour and not waste time on regrets like the man stuck in a bog who wanted first to calculate how far he had sunk without realizing that in the time spent on that he was sinking still deeper.[11]

The past is not to be lamented but can hardly be forgotten. In one of several long entries recording walks taken that summer in 1835, he writes of a favourite spot on the coast just north of Gilleleje, in the silence of which the few dear departed ones rose from the grave before me, or rather, it seemed as though they were not dead. I felt so much at ease in their midst, I rested in their embrace, and I felt as though I were outside my body and floated about with them in a higher ether – until the seagull's harsh screech reminded me that I stood alone and it all vanished before my eyes . . .[12]

Nicoline, Ane, Petrea, Niels Andreas – it sounds almost as though, instead of wishing they could rejoin him, his wish was that he could be with them. They had all died in the last two years while Kierkegaard had been reluctantly focusing on his theology studies. No wonder these began to seem irrelevant and his home empty. Death had meant more than the departure of the dear ones; it had also removed the insulation of numbers and left those three disparate male survivors too close to each other to be able to say they really shared a home. So home had to be somewhere else – on the streets and in the mind. One notes the apprentice writer's style. Rather than agonized recordings of distressing events, the entries here acquire a literary sheen and can be read as exercises in a talent with which their writer hopes to make his mark in the future.

It *was* a talent that would serve him well not only *as* a writer but as a self-confirming form of activity that brought its own rewards, including, importantly, alleviation of his depression. Much later, he was to say that it was his intellectual work that had kept his melancholia at bay.[13] By that time, though, the causes of depression were occasioned more directly by the 'battle' that he now predicted. Yet even now his studies, however fragmented, must surely have helped to keep the 'dear departed' from interfering too intrusively with his thoughts of what was to come.

Søren's studies during these five years had predictably disproved headmaster Nielsen's prediction that he would come to resemble his single-minded eldest brother. He had chosen theology because it was expected of him – not least by his father – and being a broad subject, with philosophy, in a broad sense, as a component, it turned out to be a convenient platform on which further options might be entertained. The school-leaving examination had posed no problems. It included science, and Søren ended with good grades and with distinction in Greek. The first part of the two-stage university propaedeutic examination in Greek, Hebrew, history and lower mathematics was passed with distinction in mathematics, and in the second part he received distinction in all subjects: theoretical and practical philosophy, physics and higher mathematics. A final preliminary before settling down to his studies had been quickly dealt with. After four days in uniform, Søren was summarily removed from the roll of the King's Lifeguard as unfit for service.

That, once his studies were started, his initial focus should be on philosophy was an accident of the curriculum. His studies brought him under the influence of two men who, before and after the Gilleleje summer, became Kierkegaard's intellectual and moral mainstays. They were diametrically opposed personalities. Frederick Christian Sibbern was a serious-minded thinker who wrote in a discursive and conscientiously painstaking style, while Poul Martin Møller was a stylist able in his concise prose to capture the foibles and tendencies of the age. Where Sibbern was a true scholar, Møller's reputation rested lightly on a talent for pregnant aphorism, though also as an inspiring teacher. A man of experience, in Møller's earlier days, he had been ship's chaplain on the China seas. He was also author of an unfinished novel, *A Danish Student's Tale*, chapters of which he had narrated to the Student Union while Søren was still in school. It foreshadowed Kierkegaard's own focus on individuality. Several other Kierkegaardian motifs are found in Møller, from whose *Strøtanker* (Aphorisms) his student would also take the title of his doctoral (at the time Magister's) dissertation 'On the Concept of Irony'.

Sibbern, who lectured in psychology as well as in logic and philosophy, was a kindly but strict and dependable confidant at whose home Kierkegaard would be a frequent visitor during the following years; but it was Møller who made the deeper impression. He exuded a mixture of unhappiness and enthusiasm, the latter for antiquity in particular, and he had a poetic talent that personified an optimism and a spiritual strength that Søren must at the time have felt lacking in himself. Møller would also provide a constructive foil to Kierkegaard's disposition to split and divide. Sibbern could report that Møller, on his deathbed, had chided Kierkegaard for being 'so thoroughly polemical it's just awful'.[14]

Aesthetics was the subject that first began seriously to engage their young student. Here too the polemics were to play a part, although it took time for them to take shape. Aesthetics was a broad subject that encompassed the role of various genres in the fulfilment of human life and, if not philosophy as such, it was an important element in the 'speculative' philosophy of the Hegelians. In Kierkegaard's early days as a student, it was this that had taken a hold in Danish intellectual circles, which had hitherto tended towards the Romantic theology and metaphysics of Schleiermacher. Møller, before being appointed in Copenhagen, had earlier introduced Hegel to Norway, though he would later dissociate himself from him. Another Copenhagen notable, perhaps Copenhagen's most versatile intellectual, Johan Ludwig Heiberg, was an effective popularizer of Hegelian thought.

Not all Kierkegaard's attendances at the university are recorded, but he had already begun accumulating a considerable library that kept him busy at home. There is, however, a record of his attendance at Sibbern's lectures on the 'Philosophy of Christianity' in the winter term of his third academic year (1833–4). These lectures included a criticism of Hegel's philosophy of religion for incorporating Christianity within the philosophical system, a matter we saw Kierkegaard had noted and defended in a long journal entry from October the following year.

So much for the run-up to the Gilleleje Testament: its promise of a 'battle' soon proved not to be empty. That autumn, Søren heard that a student colleague was to give a paper at the Student Union on press censorship, and chose to write a response to it. It is unclear how much the subject itself occupied him, but at this stage of his life it was enough for him that it engaged others. Replying would give him an opportunity to be heard and welcomed outside the confines of tea rooms and his hollowed-out home. He informed the seniors of the Union of his intention to 'give a reading'.[15] Johannes Ostermann, the colleague to whom he would respond, gave him his manuscript, and Kierkegaard got down to work.

It was at the Student Union that Poul Møller had recited three chapters of his unfinished novel several years earlier. By now political events had begun to play a larger part, and the premises afforded a meeting place where voices raised for and against the

Kierkegaard's teacher and friend, Professor F. C. Sibbern.

established order could be heard. Due to these wider functions, the union had close ties with newspaper journalism, made all the more significant in this case because the topic was to be freedom of the press. Denmark had been slower than other countries to make the constitutional reforms then agitating Europe, and when the newly founded liberal paper *Fædrelandet* (The Fatherland) published proposals for reform, a nervous monarch had taken from the press its right of judicial appeal. Ostermann had applauded the press for its fight against censorship. Kierkegaard, in the typical debating format of the time, would 'oppose' Ostermann's case for reform.

With his lively but – as Sibbern related – somewhat 'sarcastic' demeanour, Kierkegaard was no stranger to the Union or to his audience. To them, however, the venue would be quite untypical. 'Usually in the company of somebody' and 'constantly on the street or in public places' was how Ostermann himself could recall Kierkegaard.[16] His home no longer a sanctuary, from early student days Søren had sought at the Student Union the contact he missed, not just for the company, but to use his peers as foils for the thoughts that his voracious reading constantly put into his head. The young man with unruly hair stumbling along half-sideways in eager conversation, sometimes stopping altogether to stress a point, was by now a familiar sight in Copenhagen. On that day, 28 November 1835, the large audience would be curious to see how this peripatetic tea room intellectual would perform before an audience. Could he stick to the point for a whole hour?

The audience were doubtless surprised at the down-to-earth nature of the text from which Kierkegaard read. Indeed, its main purpose seems to have been to shed light on certain facts about the recent journalistic past, facts that would indicate how misleading Ostermann's optimistic claims for the liberal press had been a fortnight earlier. This aesthete had done his homework. He recapitulated the press's recent activity and found that, instead of being anything like a reform movement with a unified front, the radical press had merely been reacting to a well-prepared defence by the establishment. If they really wanted change, they should hold a steady course: 'in any new development your eye must be constantly on the compass and . . . it is no good travelling in Zealand with a map of France.'[17] In other words, perhaps things in Denmark are not as bad as the liberal press would have it, and in any case they differed greatly from the situation in Paris in July 1830.

But it was hardly politics that drew Kierkegaard to the lectern. Ostermann himself assumed that the topic was 'a matter of indifference' to Kierkegaard and that he would have *defended* the press had someone sufficiently important opposed it.[18] They knew each other well enough for personal animosity not to be at stake, but there were wider issues. In the wake of the Romantic movement, the literati had high standing as custodians of the human spirit. Just as estate owners, bureaucrats and clergymen could sense the dangers that critical journalism presented for their positions in society, so too were influential men of letters wary of this danger to their high status. The doyen of letters in Denmark was the aforementioned Heiberg, a man of prodigious enterprise and ability, who dominated the literary scene, not least by owning and editing the most influential literary and philosophical journals.

The previous December, Kierkegaard had published a brief article that seemed designed mainly to find favour with Heiberg's influential coterie. A welcome at the Heiberg salon, hosted by Heiberg's wife – Denmark's leading actress Johanne Luise Heiberg (née Pätges) – would be tantamount to being received at court. It is true that Kierkegaard, in the privacy of the Gilleleje Testament, had remarked that coteries were for losers and tended to efface the identities of those with egos too weak to resist the conformity they typically induced ('how often we see people who from spiritual laziness live on the crumbs that fall from other people's tables'), but the very style of the declaration breathed urgent literary ambition. The budding writer would dearly love the imprimatur of an invitation so long as he took care 'like a gnat' not to come 'too close to the flame'.[19] Of course, once he had a hearing, Kierkegaard could rail against the coteries openly and upstage the very doyen himself by undermining the basis on which Heiberg supported his role as spiritual custodian.

This indeed was the veiled import of the talk – which took two weeks to prepare – that Kierkegaard managed to wrap in a rejoinder focused on a single newspaper, naturally enough *not* one of Heiberg's.

Heiberg was an elitist, but a highly accomplished one – among his many achievements were his vaudeville writings and works on philosophy. It helped his position that he could combine the two. Two years before Ostermann's talk and Kierkegaard's response, Heiberg had published an elegantly written monograph, *On the Significance of Philosophy for the Present*. Here Hegel's philosophy was presented as alone capable of bringing order back to a morally and politically disintegrating world. What the age needed was philosophy. But here at home it also needed Heiberg the artist. At first glance, Hegel's philosophy seemed to gainsay that. In his philosophical system, religion and art were both false anticipations of the eternal idea. But, as Heiberg pointed out, religion and art can provide anticipations that are less false as well as more so. In many ages, as Hegel himself insisted, art, religion and also philosophy itself express only the inadequate form in which that age has historically appropriated the 'idea' that philosophy promises to bring to fulfilment. They are indeed merely *that age's* idea of itself. Art, too, can speak inadequately to its own age. If, for instance, a work of art speaks only to the individual, then in terms of the Hegelian 'idea', this is a false anticipation of its promise of the universal synthesis to which the Hegelian philosophy now shows us we all belong. It is, therefore, decadent art to that extent. To be true to its age, art must be that age speaking adequately to itself, and it does so best when it lets the idea reveal itself in art's own way:

Johan Ludwig Heiberg (1791–1860), playwright, philosopher and doyen of Denmark's literary circles.

'Here it is merely a matter of opening our eyes to that which we already see without knowing it, of unfolding our consciousness and showing ourselves what it contains.'[20] Those able to bring the idea to consciousness have an essential role to play.

Remarkably, Heiberg had two years previously completed a treatise on aesthetics based on Hegel's lectures on aesthetics. These were lectures that Heiberg had actually attended, and the treatise, which Heiberg left unpublished because he was not wholly satisfied with it, was ready on his desk six years before the (posthumous)

Johanne Louise Heiberg (Pätges) (1812–1890), Denmark's leading actress acclaimed at the Royal Theatre and wife of Johan Ludwig Heiberg.

publication of Hegel's *Lectures on Fine Art*. Since, in Hegelian aesthetics, comedy comes out on top, Heiberg's vaudevillian talent showed him to be at art's apex, something that he could enjoy without making too much of the Hegelian assertion that comedy was also the culmination of the contribution of art to the Hegelian goal of true self-understanding, a task then first to be taken over by religion and then grasped finally in the categories of philosophy. Comedy brings individuality into focus but exposes the limitations that immediacy and reflection impose on each other. The irony in comedy is that it engenders an awareness of the limitations as they are – that is, as actual limitations – and yet comedy (in the quite sophisticated form of vaudeville at the time) is the art form that opens the way in actual experience to a sense of perfected being. What Heiberg conveniently omits is the Hegelian notion that before the 'idea' can take on its rational form in philosophy, it is the 'aesthetic' of religion that now takes over the burden of giving us a sense of wholeness.

Kierkegaard's interest in aesthetics at the time was drawing him towards a constructive notion of personal unity – that is to say, 'individuality' – based on aesthetic categories, but in a sense of 'aesthetic' that is not exclusive to art. In his response to Ostermann's talk, he refers to the individual life as the 'point of entry' for the form of the 'idea'. This would later be developed into the idea of an 'aesthetic view of life', with its own development from immediacy to a reflective form that implies both its apotheosis and downfall. Here, however, Kierkegaard was intent on expanding Heiberg's amendment to what in Hegel appears to be a disparaging of art by allowing not just art *about* life but *life itself* to be the locus for the emergence of the 'idea'. When taken together with the observation that 'life itself is not something abstract but something extremely individual', we see that what Kierkegaard is implying here is that 'form' has to be drawn not from the quick fix of art – however great – but from the resources of life as one finds it. Form is not something one can *impose* on oneself, let alone on the world one lives in:

> Just as a leap backward is wrong (something the age is inclined on the whole to acknowledge), so also is a leap forward wrong – both of them because a natural development does not develop

in leaps, and life's earnestness will ironize every such experiment, even if for the moment it succeeds.[21]

Those of Kierkegaard's readers for whom 'Kierkegaard' and 'the leap' are synonymous will be surprised at that quotation, but it is crucial to note that the 'leap' that later enters the writings was a hard decision to maintain an already-established form when reason can offer no basis for doing so – in other words, a matter not of new beginnings but of staying the course. No doubt on this November day the audience would have been more attentive to the young man's uncanny knack for finding and even creating weaknesses in the opponent's text, and above all, opportunities to score points, than to this first sketch of an existential conception of human fulfilment.

Facing facts and not obscuring them by presenting them in a false light was Kierkegaard's ostensible theme. His title was 'Our Journal Literature: A Study of Nature in the Light of Midday'. The talk exploited the censorship issue to illustrate the danger of imposing untried forms upon an established order. These 'unreal' and abstract forms were being treated as unquestioned growth points whose assistance to progress was prevented only by external factors, the latter including tradition itself. Instead of waiting to see how a new idea actually works, one 'dwells on its first entrance on the world scene . . . [and] wants people from East and West to come and worship it in its swaddling clothes'. Anticipating a later habit of scriptural allusion, Kierkegaard says there is wishful thinking in this, a factual grain of mustard seed being made into a 'mighty tree'.[22] It is the same, he says, as the way in which early morning light is preferred by landscape painters because at that time the play of light and shadow picks out nothing in particular and thereby imparts an 'especially favourable overall impression'.[23] To see the facts for what they are, you need to expose them to the light of high noon. Ostermann later recalled that the talk had been 'rather heavy going'. But it 'bore the hallmark of [Kierkegaard's] unique intellectual talents' and was received with 'great applause'.[24]

It is clear that the real opponent was not Ostermann, nor in any explicit way Heiberg, but a politician. Orla Lehmann was the foremost spokesman for liberalism and future leader of the Liberal Party. At that time he, too, was looking for an audience, in his case those supporting opposition to Denmark's absolute monarchy. In 1842 he would be jailed for three months for suggesting that farmers had not been favoured by that system.[25] So Lehmann was bound to take an interest in this debate, and he joined in the duly pseudonymous newspaper exchange that followed, in which Kierkegaard signed himself 'B'. Eventually responding under his own name, though patronizingly, Lehmann welcomed any opportunity for sharpening the liberal press's own criticism of the government and conceded (as had been pointed out) that the Danish reform movement had lacked its O'Connell, let alone a Luther or a Moses. But he took exception to Mr B's identification of the whole reform effort with single persons and these in turn with the editor and staff of a single newspaper. When Kierkegaard, too, eventually responded under his own name, the exchange attracted too much attention for a politician, and Lehmann diplomatically withdrew from the fray. However, there was a feeling abroad, voiced by Kierkegaard's school friend Peter Rørdam, that at least one reform had been made:

> There has been a change in the Student Union. Their chieftain and leader, Lehmann, has fallen, totally beaten . . . and the victor is the younger Kierkegaard, who now writes in *Flyvende Post* under the label B.[26]

Kierkegaard had made his mark. *København's Flyvende Post* (Copenhagen's Flying Post) was edited and owned by Heiberg. Not only was he welcomed in the Heiberg home, Søren Kierkegaard was

Peter Martin Orla Lehmann (1810–1870), journalist, politician and key figure in Denmark's parliamentary government who spent a period in prison in 1842 for his advocacy of freedom of the press. Portrait by Elisabeth Jerichau Baumann, 1948.

accorded the honour of being able to invite himself to its soirées. He had been given an audience and he had found one. More than that, he had established a pattern of polemical writing that would be his hallmark for the next twenty years.

## 4

# Faust and the Feminine

In a letter (probably never sent but intended for other purposes) to a cousin in Brazil, Kierkegaard admits to being interested in too many things and 'not decisively in anything'. Peter Wilhelm Lund was a palaeontologist, twice a gold-prize winner at the university for dissertations on vivisection and crustaceans and with a doctorate from Kiel (then in Denmark). Kierkegaard wishes he had something he could investigate with a passion similar to that of Lund in faraway Brazil. It was a wish that would be fulfilled later in what Kierkegaard referred to as a 'domestic journey' from his own 'consciousness' to the 'preconditions of original sin'.[1] But there was much uneven ground to be covered before he could even contemplate such a journey.

There is no indication that Kierkegaard's despair was less following that summer's self-confession. At home again, he found himself disenchanted with the house religion: 'Christianity deprives people of their manhood.'[2] Nor was the atmosphere there conducive to the free unfolding of any other idea that he might be willing to live and die for. Josiah Thompson has given a graphic description of the three loners sharing their unshared lives under one roof:

Michael Pedersen, melancholy and crotchety; Peter Christian, stolid and self-righteous. Søren, acerbic and inwardly preoccupied – huddled together in the many rooms of the house that now was too large for them. From the rooms on the first floor the father could hear Peter's students climbing the stairs when they came for their tutorials. The two sons had rooms side by side on the second floor. In Peter's there was a desk by the window where the students sat while the Doctor (so-called because of his Göttingen degree [which nevertheless could not qualify Peter for a professorship]) corrected their Latin compositions or discussed a point of theology. And off to the side lay Søren reading. One of the students later recalled that only once had Søren ever ventured to interject an opinion.[3]

The family home would be Søren's for another nine months. In the first period, from January to midsummer following the summer break at Gilleleje, the journals express a growing instability that – over the course of the late winter and spring – comes close to a nervous breakdown. There is a gradual focusing on the figure of Faust and other icons of legend.

In the Gilleleje Testament, Kierkegaard had toyed with the idea of becoming a public prosecutor; the world of jurisprudence would 'sharpen [his] mind on life's many complications'. Insight into the 'organism of criminal life' would reveal life 'in all its darker sides'. There is a touch of Faust in this, but he then adds that, even here, there is room for a 'community spirit'. This was a theme Kierkegaard had also touched on in earlier musings on the then-popular 'master-thief' figure known from antiquity. Fascination with the life of crime once led Kierkegaard to confess to his 'enormous desire to carry out an actual theft, and then live with his bad conscience and in fear of discovery'.[4] It was a fantasy later shared by Nietzsche.

Kierkegaard's fascination with this typical boyhood myth might be attributed to his 'never [having] had the joy of childhood'.[5] But the master-thief theme can attract anyone with a tendency to feel outside things. With a superior grasp of society and its ills, but ready at personal risk to challenge the system even if by himself

Kierkegaard's family home on Nytorv, demolished in 1908.

he cannot change it, the master-thief is the misfit's perfect alibi. The 22-year-old Kierkegaard sees the master-thief as a product of the 'popular class' (*Folkeklasse*), suggesting something like the Hegelian master–slave dialectic, where the deprived give a more faithful picture of their society than that found in its own official portrait. Early on, Kierkegaard had pointed to Till Eulenspiegel, the inveterate prankster of a North German (and then also Danish) folk tale, who was also of the 'lower' class.[6] Although Eulenspiegel was no criminal, the indiscriminate and ubiquitous nature of his bawdy humour anticipates a theme that Kierkegaard, with more elevated support from the anti-Enlightenment thinker Johann Georg Hamann ('the greatest humorist in Christianity'), was to maintain throughout his writings: the all-embracing humour that attaches to everything once its futility is seen in the light of an ideal that nothing measures up to.[7] As for the master-thief, when caught and charged, not unlike Socrates (whose deft removal of people's ill-based opinions might well qualify him for the part), he treats the proceedings as though the court were on trial rather than himself – the misfit's perfect turnaround as well as alibi.

A normal childhood was not the only thing of which Kierkegaard sensed that he had been deprived. It was to two embarrassed sons that Michael Pedersen came to tell of his misdeeds and why the whole family was conceived in sin. On returning from Gilleleje that summer, Søren had found his father in a self-confessional mood and not completely sober. What was revealed is not known for certain, but a late notebook entry can be read in connection with this. It says it is 'more dangerous' for a child to be brought up in the assurance that his father is a God-fearing man but for the child to see in the father a profound 'disquiet' that not even the fear of God can requite, than to have a father who is a 'freethinker' or a 'hypocrite'.[8] An undated journal entry marked '25 yrs old' refers to an earlier 'earthquake' that left Kierkegaard in pieces. He writes dramatically of a sense of death creeping up on him, with a foreboding that his father's 'advanced age' was a 'curse' rather than a 'divine blessing', and that Michael Pedersen would come to outlive them all.[9]

Could the shock be due to the silence imposed on the household on matters that inescapably come to body and mind in puberty? Søren had inherited his father's pietism but without access to the natural man. The last journal entry Kierkegaard ever made refers to the 'crime' through which he 'came into the world'. It was 'against God's will' and as befitted the crime, his punishment had been to be 'bereft of all lust for life'.[10]

This, the pietism and what had been omitted, might explain Søren's fascination with another legendary figure, Don Juan, whose lust for life manifested itself in serial seduction. Just before Ostermann's talk, Kierkegaard had attended a performance of *Don Giovanni*. The opera had made a deep impression on him; he is said to have attended every subsequent performance. Don Juan was in sharp contrast to Faust, a thinker whose intellection led him to doubt and whose monogamous fancy to the simple and unreflective Gretchen interrupted his diabolical search for knowledge. As a serial seducer, Don Juan was someone in whom the search and sex-life were one and the same. To these figures, another figure – the subject of several of Poul Møller's aphorisms – had already been added: Ahasuerus, also known as the Wandering Jew. According to the legend, Jesus had stopped at Ahasuerus' house to rest the cross. On being pushed aside by Ahasuerus, he had said, 'Truly I go away, and quickly, but you are staying until I return.'[11]

Kierkegaard had described these as the 'three great ideas representing the . . . distinct directions in which life tends outside religion'.[12] As in the prevailing Hegelian climate we would expect, they also correspond to increasing distances from religion. Ahasuerus represents the blank denial that Kierkegaard in *The Sickness Unto Death* would later call 'the height of despair'. It would also seem the height of departure, but then, in a note written just after his paper to the Student Union, Kierkegaard has Ahasuerus change places with Faust: 'We shouldn't forget that Don Juan has to be grasped lyrically (and therefore with music); the Wandering Jew epically, and Faust dramatically.'[13] Music comes lowest on Heiberg's scale of aesthetic expression and drama highest because, as noted earlier, it synthesizes immediacy and reflection. The Wandering Jew, an ascetic, is now placed against Don Juan and his obsessive lust for life, with Faust then combining lust with reflection. Everything seems now nicely Heibergian but without loss of a sense of a direction away from religion. Don Juan simply doesn't want to know about it since it would interfere with his continual search for sensual pleasure; Ahasuerus knows about religion but unreflectively pushes it aside, while for the knowledge-hungry Faust, it is reflection that leads to his doubt and to all that follows.

The Faustian role seems to be the one that Kierkegaard found himself closest to taking on. The rejection of religion or faith can be understood in two ways: either as recognition of religion as an 'extra' to be disposed of since it cannot help in the human project and is not something out of which to build societies or homes (in the way that the Moravians and Michael Pedersen believed) and certainly not something for a Faust who wants to extend knowledge beyond the human; or else it is a cure for those who agonize over life and discover that a purely human project has no value, yet, being so 'radical', the cure is one that we 'put off as long as possible'.[14] At first, Kierkegaard had wanted to *save* religion from philosophy. Now, with a touch of the Mephistophelean, he was leaning in the other direction. It looks as if he had found out how far his wit could take him as a useful means of defence and provocation, but it had somehow emptied him. In the early months of 1836, he had been living on that wit in newspaper articles and at parties, but the journal entries are strained and terse: 'Damn and hell, I can abstract from everything but *not from myself*; I can't even forget myself when I sleep.'[15] One entry takes up the distinction between irony and humour but both depend on 'not coming to terms with the world'. Another says simply 'the ubiquity of wit', while yet another sees its limits:[16]

I have just come back from a party where I was the life and soul. Witticisms flowed from my lips. Everyone laughed and admired me – but I left, yes, that dash should be as long as the radii of the earth's orbit ——————— and I wanted to shoot myself.[17]

Naturally, the Faust label doesn't quite fit; there is no deal with the devil. On the other hand, Kierkegaard would later be plagued by the thought that he had taken on a superman's role without first asking God. The more obvious parallel is a background of years-long study with little progress and losing both himself and his faith in the process. And then there was to be a Gretchen. If he could suppress the humour and the irony enough to come to terms with the world – not on *its* terms of course, for that would mean collapsing back *into* the world – but with the help of an Archimedean point outside it, then he would be ready to resume his father's religion but with a deeper understanding of its meaning and demands.

Yes, Regine – that delightful, and intelligent young lady whose look of adoration Kierkegaard would later describe as capable of 'moving stones'; her sheer presence would tempt him to stay with the world on its own terms.[18] And yet she was not the first young lady to attract him. A frequently quoted journal entry goes,

> Today too (8 May) I was trying to forget myself, though not with any noisy to-do – that substitute doesn't help, but by going out to Rørdam's to talk with Bolette, and by trying (if possible) to make that devil-wit stay at home, that angel who with blazing sword, as I deserve, interposes himself between me and every innocent girlish heart – when you caught up with me, O God, I thank you for not letting me instantly lose my mind – never have I been more afraid of that; so be thanked for once more bending your ear to me.[19]

Kierkegaard had been visiting his theologian friend Peter Rørdam, who lived with his widowed mother. On that day, 7 May 1837, her three daughters Elisabeth, Emma and Bolette were hosts to their fifteen-year-old friend Regine Olsen. Many years later, Regine could recall how this young man had presented himself without warning and made a 'very strong impression' on her.

He 'spoke unceasingly', indeed his speech 'practically poured forth and was extremely captivating'. Because Kierkegaard had tried to cross out the reference to Bolette in his journal, the published version led everyone, including Regine, later to believe that the high-strung journal entry referred to his first meeting with her. But it was the 22-year-old Bolette, 'a very beautiful and sensible girl' according to her brother, who had first captured Kierkegaard's interest.[20] Age-wise she would have been a more suitable match, and Kierkegaard later acknowledged that he and Bolette had made an 'impression' on each other, for which he felt a certain 'responsibility' towards her – 'even if in all innocence and purely intellectually'.[21] Indeed, earlier that year Kierkegaard wrote, 'what is friendship without intellectual exchange?'[22] With Bolette, he could employ his wit and humour in an intelligent exchange with a young woman without any hint of the Don Juan. On the other hand, her evident appreciation might excite just those feelings that his father had never owned to. Or was it the presence of the attractive young visitor? Or even the entire feminine assembly including a mother? Was there more than a hint here of the eternal feminine that put Goethe's Faust off course? For a moment, the unceasingly productive feminine might eclipse the masculine God of unchangeable severity on that heath, and now at home. Losing his mind? What mind? His own mind, the mind that he had made up about staying securely in the cloister. Here he was, for safety's sake, hanging on grimly to that religious perspective. Soon after there came another entry:

> Today, again, the same performance – Still, I managed to get out to R[ørdam's] – my God, why should this tendency awaken just now – O, how alone I feel! – O, damn that arrogance of being content to stand on my own – everyone will now despise me – O, but you, my God, do not let go of me – let me live and make myself better . . .[23]

This entry too was crossed out. The next time the name Rørdam appears in the journal is Sunday 9 July 1837, when, walking back from Frederiksberg, Kierkegaard stopped off in the gardens and noted,

> I stand like a *solitary* spruce, egoistically self-enclosed and pointing toward what is higher, casting no shadow, and only the wood dove builds its nest in my branches . . . Sunday (9 July 37) in Frederiksberg Gardens after calling at the Rørdam place.[24]

Kierkegaard had moved into a rented apartment. In the autumn, he would begin teaching Latin at his old school. It was as if the umbilical cord with his home had been cut. Freed of the ghosts

The School of Civic Virtue (Borgerdydskolen) on Klareboderne, attended by Kierkegaard and his brothers and where he taught Latin in the autumn of 1837.

J. V. Gertner, *Hans Lassen Martensen* (1808–1884), 1854.

of the past and the father's destructive faith, he may have felt more Faustian than he wanted – that is, the Faust of whom Kierkegaard says that his willingness to familiarize himself with evil is not to feel *above* such things ('only the petty bourgeois do that') but to have 'all the sluice gates of sin open within his breast, the whole kingdom of boundless possibilities'.[25] An addendum, 'this will not be enough; his expectations will deceive him', suggests someone on the brink but facing religion once more, waiting only for something to jolt him into faith.

His self-confidence had already received several blows. More were to come. Yet another death had occurred in the family home, that of his brother's wife in July 1837 after only two years of marriage. Closer to home, in another sense there had been still another loss: 'Oh, how unhappy I am – Martensen has written a treatise on Lenau's Faust!'[26] What a disappointment for someone who had been working on Faustian themes since 1835.[27] Worse was the fact that Hans Lassen Martensen was the closest Kierkegaard felt anyone in Copenhagen could be to being a rival. Their adversarial relationship had begun in earlier student years when Martensen, who was five years older, offered to tutor Kierkegaard on Schleiermacher and was met with what he later described as an 'irresistible urge to sophistry' and 'hair-splitting games'.[28] The bad feeling was to last until Kierkegaard's death, when Martensen was Denmark's newly appointed primate. Kierkegaard's – to some ears – strangely belated polemic against Hegelianism may even have been prompted more than anything by the popularity of a lecture series on Hegel that Martensen gave on returning in 1836 from an extended study tour of Germany. Kierkegaard, who attended the lectures, wrote that Martensen gave his listeners the impression they 'could swallow everything in half a year'.[29] It was not only the implication that something so comprehensive could be ingested in such a short time; it was also the idea of philosophy becoming a vogue and by implication easy to grasp and chat about. But there must additionally have been a measure of jealousy on Kierkegaard's part towards this astute, serious and cosmopolitan young man; the popularity would be irksome enough. Things were not to improve when Martensen was chosen to fill a vacancy left by Poul Møller.

That represented yet another blow. Ill for some time, Poul Møller died the following spring, on 13 March 1838, aged only 44. Kierkegaard writes, 'Again such a long time has gone in which I have been unable to rally myself for the least thing – I must now make another attempt at it' and then announces, 'Poul Møller is dead.'[30] If Kierkegaard saw in Møller's writing a model for his own developing talents, it was without doubt to the man himself, with his spontaneous and nonconformist personality, that he was really devoted.[31] Soon after his mentor's death, Kierkegaard tried

Poul Martin Møller (1794–1838), Kierkegaard's teacher and mentor, on his deathbed.

his hand at a review of a recent novel by Hans Christian Andersen, *Only a Fiddler*. When the review was completed in mid-July, Heiberg disliked the style and refused it. After a friend, Hans Peter Holst, had rewritten the review 'or rather translated it from Latin into Danish', it appeared in September under the title *From the Papers of One Still Living*.[32] The added signature goes, 'Published Against His Will by S. Kierkegaard.'

In the preface, Kierkegaard writes that he takes it all back 'into the womb' in order to let it 'subside once more in the twilight from which it emerged'. That might be because many of the ideas were Møller's and should be returned to where they came from; the borrowings included a 'life-view', of which the work makes much in order to present Andersen as someone in whose work it is singularly lacking. More likely, it indicates a nascent reluctance on the part of Kierkegaard to write under his own name, suggesting an alter ego, or even a still-more-secluded self, behind the pen. Kierkegaard spoke of this separation as leaving him 'free', but free to do what? To arrive at his own life-view, perhaps, and let *it* come to expression in his works. In criticizing Andersen for giving too much of himself, Kierkegaard says the 'genesis' of his novels is more 'amputation' than 'production'.[33]

The review, the delay in whose arrival and especially its content caused Andersen much torment, appeared only a month after a still more fateful death, that of Michael Pedersen Kierkegaard. It occurred after an episode recorded in a note that is not only dated but timed (10.30 a.m. on 19 May), and in which Kierkegaard says that the episode gave him 'indescribable joy'. Whatever caused the euphoria, and how long it lasted in a man of such reflection, is not revealed. But something had tipped him back into the sanctuary of a religious perspective. From July of that year, 1838, we read of a determination to 'come into a far more intimate relation with Christianity'.[34] The December before, he had already wondered whether, should he ever become an 'earnest Christian', his 'deepest shame' might be that he left it so long and had to 'try everything else first'.[35] However earnest a Christian he had become at that point, one result of this turnaround was that he would now be on better terms with his father and brother. Having moved out of the family home, he was thinking of coming back.

But Michael Pedersen had been ailing for some time and died on 9 August 1838 in his 82nd year. Kierkegaard had written a few weeks earlier, 'How I thank you, Father in heaven, for having kept here on earth, for a time like the present when my need for it was so great, an earthly father . . .'[36] Now he writes of the death as a 'last act of love' for the son, even a 'sacrifice'.[37] It was in any case a release from a subtle form of captivity that had kept Søren from finding his own strengths. Michael Pedersen was not unaware of his inhibiting effect on his son. In one account, he had said, 'It would actually be good for you if I were dead; then you might yet make something of yourself: you won't do that as long as I am alive.'[38] Sibbern, on hearing of Michael Pedersen's death, had told Søren, 'Now you will never get your theology degree.'[39] But of course, for Sibbern, getting the degree and making something of oneself would be much the same thing. Since the oldest son had taken care of the academics, the enterprising and imaginative Michael Pedersen might well have entertained less conventional prospects for his youngest son's future.

Kierkegaard disagreed with Sibbern: 'Had father lived on, I would never have got [the theology degree].' He also agreed with his father over the fact that the large amount of money he would now inherit would be of no help, but for a different reason. His father, according to Søren, thought he would 'drink it and dream it away', but 'with my sharp mind, and my melancholia, and then with money – oh, what favourable conditions for developing all the torments of self-torture in my heart.'[40] The money was nevertheless very useful on the journey to make something of himself, which was about to begin. He could also now defend his father's faith without feeling that it was merely to please him. Yet it is also possible that Søren might have felt that he now owed it to himself to find some way of defending that faith in his own way, one that might not please his father. Whatever the truth was, he got down to work and, with almost superhuman energy, managed in short order to absorb the curriculum of the subject he hated most.

Kierkegaard called the time he spent in this pursuit a 'parenthesis' – the longest that he had experienced.[41] It began with his moving into another apartment with a fellow student, and later into yet another on his own, his already considerable library increasing with each move. It was a time of trial, but something had helped him to work through what a confidant described on his behalf as this 'driest of disciplines'.[42] Amid memorizing the dates of popes, absorbing reflections on true and false Christianity, and understanding the role of philosophy, the image of his heart's 'sovereign mistress' intruded.

As her name suggests, the sovereign mistress was Regine. The now-wealthy young man was exposed to a disturbing dream, one that in the midst of the academic drudgery called for words. On 2 February 1839 Regine was immortalized in this much-quoted journal entry:

> You, Sovereign mistress of my heart ['Regina'], hidden in the deepest privacy of my breast, in my most brimming thoughts on life, there, where it is just as far to heaven as to hell – unknown divinity! Oh, can I really believe the poets' tales that when one sees the beloved for the first time one believes one has seen her long before; that all love, like all knowledge, is recollection; that love too has its prophecies, its types, its myths, its Old Testament in the single individual. Everywhere, in every girl's face, I see a trace of your beauty, but it seems to me that I would have to have all girls in order to extract *your* beauty from all of theirs; that I'd have to circumnavigate the earth to find that continent which I lack, and that the deepest secrecy of my entire 'I' nevertheless points to it as its pole; – and in the next moment you are so near to me, so present, so powerfully making my spirit whole, that I am transfigured in my own eyes and feel that here is a good place to be . . . You blind god of love! You who see in secret, will you tell me openly? Shall I find what I am seeking here in this world, shall I experience the *conclusion* of all my life's eccentric premises, shall I *enclose* you in my arms – or
>
> ### Does the order say: onward?
>
> Have you gone ahead, you my *longing*; do you summon me, transfigured, from another world? Oh, I would cast everything aside to become light enough to follow you.[43]

When Regine's adorable image overprinted that of the appealing Bolette is unclear. Nor is there any record of social contact during this period. Kierkegaard would claim nine years later that his mind was already set on her before the death of his father. Regine's 'existence' had been 'entwining itself' around his own all the while he was reading for the examination.[44] When at the beginning of July 1840 (it is said to the surprise of his fellow students) he had passed with the grade *laudabilis* (commendable), his choices had become more complex. If the Faustian period had been an attempt to recover an immediacy lost in childhood, it had failed for reasons Faust himself would have predicted. The alternative was to live in solitary dedication to the Christian ideal in the 'cloister'. A long journal entry on the difference between the 'original' Faust and a Faust who is supposed to 'represent the age' may be read as opening the way to that celibate alternative. While the first Faust 'sank into sensuality', this new Faust would want to 'withdraw from everything, forget, if he can, that he ever knew anything, and become a cowherd – or perhaps, out of curiosity, transport himself into another world'.[45] But there was Regine. Placing her in the real future would inevitably bring with it the prospect of marriage and a normal home life. Was he cut out for that? Later he made it very clear why he wasn't, but now he was less disposed to think of the obstacles.[46] After all, wasn't a theology degree a preliminary to a pastorate? Before him lay the prospect of a life combining Christian dedication with a civic responsibility that also gave room for marriage. In terms that would be familiar in the not-too-distant future, Kierkegaard would be 'realizing the universal'.

To recuperate after his exams, Kierkegaard left Copenhagen for Jutland on 19 July on a recreational trip accompanied by his servant Anders to his ancestral home. Recovery was not the sole purpose; there were friends of friends to visit. But above all, it was a pilgrimage to the small community in which Michael Pedersen Kierkegaard had grown up and had left while still a young boy.

The notes Kierkegaard made during the trip are straightforward and to the point, almost Hemingway-like, with none of the convoluted clauses and parentheses that had, up until then, cluttered his prose. Some comments speak of the hay and its aroma, of sheep and, humorously, of cows. They also have a poetic vein, as in describing a walk on the heath. It is from here that we have the earlier passage about the heath, which is 'peculiarly suited to developing spiritual strength'. Kierkegaard is said to have preached a sermon in the Sæding church, but the evidence is that he arrived too late to do that. However, in a 'solemn farewell speech', the parish priest expressed appreciation of Kierkegaard's father's gift to the church in honour of his uncle Niels Andersen Sædding. It was this uncle who had put Michael Pedersen on the road to prosperity. Kierkegaard stayed three nights with his 'impoverished aunt' in the now somewhat squalid home that Michael Pedersen had provided. It was known locally as the 'red house' because, uniquely in that area, it was built of brick rather than clay.[47] Noting that he was fated even here to meet with 'opposites', the place he visited on the very next day was 'overcrowded with counts and barons' – 'it was awful'.[48] All in all, this journey brought a fitting conclusion to a past full of shadows, though Kierkegaard toys with the possibility of it being just a little too fitting. Before departing, he wrote,

> I sit here all alone (many hours I have been just as alone but not so aware of it) and count the hours until I shall see *Sæding*. I can never recall any change in my father, and now I am to see the place where as a poor boy he tended sheep, the place for which, because of his descriptions of them, I have been so homesick. What if I were to become ill and be buried in Sæding churchyard! Strange idea. His last request to me is fulfilled – is that to be *all* that my earthly destiny amounts to? In God's name! Yet in relation to what I owed to him the task was not so paltry. I learned from him what fatherly love is, and through this

I gained a conception of divine fatherly love, the one single unshakable thing in life, the true Archimedean point.[49]

So much for the past, but as he records, it was also during this time that he had been 'angling' for Regine. At the time, she had a mutual 'understanding' with the family's presentable young house tutor; they had begun to look upon each other as potential partners. Before leaving for Jutland, Søren had lent her, or 'them', some books with certain passages to which particular attention was to be paid.[50] Only two days after returning to Copenhagen – he recalls that it was between the ninth and the end of the month – he made his own 'approaches', and on 8 September he proposed.

Even by the standards of the period, the proposal was a stilted pantomime. Meeting Regine outside her door, Søren interpreted her suggestion that they go in as 'the invitation [he] needed'. Once inside, there was talk of her playing something for him on the piano, but before she could begin, he snatched the music book away and flung it onto the piano: 'What do I care for music, it's you I want! I have wanted you for two years.' That she was 'flustered' is no surprise. She said nothing but he took the absence of a 'no' to mean 'yes' and went off directly to her father for an appointment. Counsellor Terkild Olsen also said nothing but seemed 'well disposed'. An appointment was made 'for the afternoon of the tenth', after which they were engaged. Kierkegaard claims never to have said a word to 'captivate her'. Regine Olsen, now eighteen years old, had in her silence said yes.[51] Søren Aabye Kierkegaard was 27.

To all appearances on course for a normal life, in November 1840 Kierkegaard entered the Royal Pastoral Seminary, where he would draft his own sermons and evaluate those of colleagues. Two months later, on Tuesday 12 January 1841, Kierkegaard preached his first sermon (assuming he had failed to arrive in time at Sæding the previous summer). Its text was from the letter to the Philippians (1:19–25), in which Paul speaks of his split between the earthly and the heavenly and about how, for him, Christ is life and therefore death is a gain. It was commented that the sermon had been 'very well memorized', the voice was 'clear' and the tone 'dignified and forceful'. The sermon had been prepared with 'much thought and sharp logic', although another commentator suggested that Kierkegaard made the 'struggles of the soul' sound too difficult for the average person to grasp. The language received high praise.[52]

Besides the seminar, Kierkegaard was at the same time beginning on his Magister's dissertation 'On the Concept of Irony'. A significant fact in connection with its title was that just before passing his examinations, a young theology student, Adolph Peter Adler, had defended his dissertation 'The Isolated Subject in its Most Important Forms'. Like Martensen, though less of a missionary, Adler too had returned from Germany a full-fledged Hegelian. No doubt this, and the thought that a younger man had produced and defended a dissertation before he had even begun, focused Kierkegaard's mind on objections to Hegel that had long lingered in his mind. In two remarkable journal entries written in June 1840, at about the time he was taking his examination, Kierkegaard takes up the question of the relation between metaphysics and history. Reality in Hegel is 'taken up into the Idea', but how does the Idea cope with contingency? Hegelians treat the isolated individual as an abstraction. As a good Hegelian, Adler believed that by 'overcoming' the contingencies of time and environment that form its identity in time, the individual becomes 'real'. Kierkegaard suggests, on the contrary, that these contingencies are ineluctable givens that have to be grasped for what they are. But if the isolated individual is to become other and more than an empty node on which these contingencies hang, then the finite world has to be treated as a 'divine habitation' in which their importance is subject to higher authority. Irony matters because for Hegelians, once irony has drained the world of value, the speculative idea is still there to resolve this final opposition between, on the one hand,

The 18-year-old Regine Olsen (1822–1904), in 1840, by Emil Bærentzen.

a world *without* value and, on the other, its very source. It was in the hope that the German Idealist philosopher Schelling might offer a solution of the kind Kierkegaard sought that he was to attend that famous philosopher's eagerly anticipated lectures a year later.

That would be in Berlin, when prospects of a 'normal' life had been ruthlessly set aside. Søren Kierkegaard would by then have started to become the author we know today. At this time, however, although the theme of the dissertation bore on Kierkegaard's reflections on Adler, and irony would be both tool and central topic in the authorship, the present offered more than enough to confuse any picture of the future.

Outwardly, Søren and Regine appeared to others like any ordinary happy couple. He visited her frequently, and they took walks and coach-rides, chaperoned often by Kierkegaard's teacher Sibbern, who was also taken along on visits to her home. But Sibbern was one of the first to see that things were not quite right and, knowing Kierkegaard, to realize that Regine was the one who would need Sibbern's support most. Nine years later, Kierkegaard would allege that the very day after she had said yes, he 'saw' he had 'made a mistake'.[53] Whether it was a hard fact that he could acknowledge at the time or a nasty feeling that grew into a sense of panic and the need to save himself, is hard to say. Eight years later, he was able to admit,

> In the course of half a year or less she would have torn herself to shreds. There is something spectral about me – and this is both the good and the bad in me – something that makes it impossible for anyone to endure having to see me every day and thus have a real relationship with me.[54]

Kierkegaard seems never to have been resigned to making the best of it. Perhaps from the very first he realized that it was the image of Regine and not the living person that had entwined itself in his thoughts. The imminent translation of the image into the human being brought him up short. Still, they must surely have become better acquainted in the times they found together in the year it took to complete the dissertation, and their friendship seems to have been genuine enough.

On Kierkegaard's part, there were indications from the start that it was over before it had properly begun. Normally, the fact that in the midst of his labours Kierkegaard wrote letters to her every week would be seen as an assurance that he had not lost interest. The letters, however, in many cases charming and friendly (though some contain a keen dash of poison), are literary exercises in their genre. Sometimes ecstatic and even sexually suggestive, they are totally devoid of the tenderness and immediacy one expects of a lover frustrated by having to finish a job in hand before being able to unite with the beloved. One characteristic letter reads,

> It is Indian summer, towards evening. – The little window is open, the moon swells, outdoing itself in splendor so as to eclipse the mirror image in the sea, which seems to outshine it, almost audibly – it is that wonderful. The moon flushes with rage and conceals itself in the clouds, the sea shivers – You sit on the sofa, the thoughts float far afield, your eye is fixed on nothing, infinite thoughts fade away only in the infinity of the wide heavens, everything in between is gone, it is as though you sailed in the air. And you summon the fleeting thoughts that show you an object, and if a sigh had propulsive power, if a human being was so light, so ethereal that the compressed air released by a sigh could carry him away, and indeed the more quickly the deeper the sigh – then you would be with me in that very instant.[55]

Regine certainly sensed her transportation into a higher sphere and remonstrated. Two months before the final break, at the start of what he later called a period of 'deceit', Søren began putting on a show of indifference in the hope that Regine would herself bring the engagement to an end. Søren's deep attachment to this perceptive, sensitive and totally charming young lady is beyond doubt, but the letters reveal that the only way to 'keep' her would be by returning the real person to her image. It was a muse and not a bride that he would be taking home with him after completing his labours. When that time came, he would also be leaving the home ostensibly to listen to what Schelling had to offer, but also to escape the scandal and gossip of a broken engagement.

On 29 September 1841, Søren successfully defended his dissertation after a disputation undertaken in Latin that lasted more than seven hours. A royal dispensation had allowed Kierkegaard to break with custom and permitted him to write his dissertation in Danish. Sibbern was in charge of the proceedings and also one of the official 'opponents'. Among those who spoke from the floor were Kierkegaard's brother Peter Christian and Heiberg. The committee that had judged the dissertation worthy of defence had acknowledged its intellectual quality but found it verbose and affected. There were also 'various excesses of the sarcastic and mocking sort' quite inappropriate in an academic setting, as well as some 'vulgar exaggeration'. Sibbern had wished that 'our author's idea were carried out with more precision', while Martensen, to whom Kierkegaard had shown a draft, said later that he found the style mannered and intolerably discursive. Sibbern, ever hopeful on his protégé's behalf, and thinking of the academic future, urged Kierkegaard to arrange a translation into German. But Kierkegaard had other plans.[56]

He had returned the engagement ring on 11 August, before the disputation. An accompanying letter said,

> So as not to go through more rehearsals of what must happen in any case, something that when it does happen will surely give strength, let it be done. Above all forget the one who writes this: forgive someone who whatever else he was capable of could not make a girl happy.

As an indication of Kierkegaard's plans not only for the present but for Regine's literary future, he would reproduce the letter (otherwise lost) in *Stages on Life's Way*.[57] However, the strength that it elicited in Regine at the time was not the stoic fortitude it hinted at. Instead 'she fought like a lioness' to defend the engagement. She went straight to Kierkegaard's apartment but, on not finding him there, wrote what according to him was an 'altogether despairing letter'. It begged him 'with tears and prayers (for the sake of Jesus Christ,

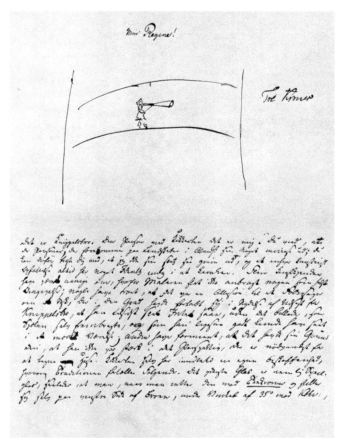

One of the ink sketches that Kierkegaard enclosed in his letters to Regine during the engagement. The text of this, dated 23 September 1840, says that it is the artist himself standing in the middle of Knippelsbro (a bridge across the inner harbour of Copenhagen) with a telescope directed at the sea fortress the Three Crowns, but with which, to one who knows how to use telescopes, one can see what one wants to see, in this case his fiancée's home.

Kierkegaard's older brother, Peter Christian (1805–1888), in 1871.

in memory of [his] dead father) not to desert her'. He could do 'anything with her, absolutely anything', and she would 'still thank [him] for the greatest of blessings'. Kierkegaard's naive reaction was to affect indifference in the hope of dampening her spirit and even make her lose interest in him. If she were to want rid of him, the onus would be on her. But that didn't happen, and Kierkegaard was to write, 'If I had not believed there was divine opposition she would have won.'[58]

It was neither scandal nor humiliation that Regine had been fighting to avoid. If her spirit aroused Søren's respect and revealed the living girl for what she was, she in turn had also got the measure of him. She understood how much of what Søren said and did lay in his personal torments. Perhaps she could empathize in ways that he could not. Her attraction to him appears to have been on several frequencies: he says that on one occasion he had to dampen her enthusiasm by reading a Mynster sermon. It was not without reason, when the final break came on 11 October, that her father, in pleading with Søren not to break the engagement, said she would otherwise die of a broken heart.

The final break came two weeks before he was to leave for Berlin. Following a wrought conversation at her home on that day, he went to the theatre and there ran into her father, a man he highly respected. When Councillor Olsen told him the break-up would be the death of her, Kierkegaard accompanied him to their home

Henriette Lund (1829–1909), devoted niece, daughter of Kierkegaard's sister Petrea Severine, who remembered the tearful farewell on Kierkegaard's leaving for Berlin in October 1841. She published her memoirs (*Recollections from Home*) in 1880.

to speak to her, though with no intention of changing course. According to her father, Regine then endured a sleepless night and when Kierkegaard visited once more, she had asked him if he would ever marry. Perhaps in an attempt at putting her off – though one cannot help but detect an unfeeling, if desperate, display of his least attractive side – he replied, 'Yes, in ten years time, when I have had my fling.' Regine took out a note concealed in her breast that he had written, quietly tore it up and said, 'So after all, you have also played a terrible game with me.'[59]

It was brother Peter Christian who worried most about the scandal for the effect it would have on the family name. Søren, with his new connections and a dissertation in his pocket, could now add his feather to the family's cap. Privately Peter Christian said that Søren was 'done for' but he would go to the Olsens and 'prove to them' that his younger brother was not a 'scoundrel'. Søren responded by saying that if Peter did that, he would 'put a bullet through his head', adding rather needlessly in his own report of the episode that this is how much it meant to him.[60] The mission was cancelled. When Søren's own family had been gathered in the old home at Nytorv, where he was once more living, they listened to the troubled Uncle Søren explain that he would be away for some time. As his niece Henriette recalled, he 'broke into a violent fit of weeping', and they all began to sob too but 'without really knowing what there was to cry about'. However, Uncle Søren quickly 'pulled himself together' and told them that he would soon be leaving for Berlin. 'With many tears', they promised to write to him since he would be 'anxious to hear how each of us was doing'.[61]

On Sunday 25 October 1841, his brother and Emil Boesen, former fellow student and the one person who could claim to be a lifelong intimate, accompanied Søren to the Swedish steamship leaving that day first for Ystad in Sweden, and then Stralsund on the Pomeranian coast. From there, he would take a stagecoach to Berlin. He had told them he planned to be away for a year and a half.

# 5

# Either/Or

According to Søren's own testimony, he spent his nights crying. During the day, though, he was his 'usual self', if not 'wittier and more flippant than ever'. It was, he said, 'necessary'.[1] Alone now with no one to deceive or expend his wit on, his loss stared him in the face: 'the only thing [he] loved', or rather, had 'deprived [himself] of' – not just Regine, but 'in [people's] eyes my word as a gentleman . . . and that in which I always have and, without fear of this blow, always shall place my honour, my joy, my pride – being faithful . . .'[2] In a cabin 'rocked by the pitching and rolling of a steamship', his 'soul' was 'as turbulent as his body'. He was also reading the Danish poet and playwright Adam Oehlenschläger's fantasy *Aladdin or the Wonderful Lamp*. With the engagement in mind, he noted down some lines:

> Not I alone, my R., but . . . all the various willing servants within me that respond to your beck and call, a servant for your every wish, and if possible ten for each . . . but in me all these unite in one genie of the ring, who unlike the one who appeared before Aladdin, is not bound in you by an external and accidental tie, but with the longing of my entire soul, for did not I myself bring you the ring that I obey.[3]

When Kierkegaard was to return to Copenhagen four-and-a-half months later and considerably sooner than he predicted, he had written or drafted large portions of *Either/Or*. A work that would be his best-seller and well over seven hundred pages long, its references to the broken engagement are more than clear. He was to say later that he wrote it for 'her sake'.[4] But there are various ways of reading that remark, and appropriately enough for a work with that title, there are two opposite views that can be helpful starters. From one vantage point, several clear messages to Regine are enclosed in a vast envelope of lavish exercises of a newly discovered poetic talent, one in which he looks forward to his own bright future as an author. From the opposite view, it is a literary presentation of philosophical themes relevant to its author's private life with thoughts of penance, but which he hopes and feels will be of general interest. The references to his own life may be incidental but conveniently serve an extra-authorial purpose. The pseudonyms help to ensure that the work can serve an edifying purpose without readers calling to mind the biographical reasons for the themes becoming topical for this particular author.

There is a factor missing here that provides a middle way. Kierkegaard later (in 1849) described his authorship as having been his own 'education'.[5] Whether by becoming more focused, altering course or taking more into account, the positions expressed in the writings undergo changes that may also be seen as alterations in the author himself. We can well allow for the obvious possibility – to be acknowledged as fact – that a later pseudonym came to express a point of view more stringent than anything he himself aspired to represent. But that acknowledgement itself was still part of a development in which his writing *became* his life, in the sense that it was the principal medium of its development as he saw it. As for the pseudonyms, several commentators have pointed out that rather than pseudonymity affording a cover, it offers an author greater freedom of self-disclosure than any duly signed autobiography. Kierkegaard could also escape the comments and questions of his contemporaries and even respond to critics under the same or another pseudonym. In any case, he seems to have believed that the development that his writings trace was one whose aims others, and above all Regine, could, in principle, appreciate. For him, it had to do with a journey towards a proper relationship to a personal God. But we also recall that itinerary for a planned 'domestic' journey from his own 'consciousness' to the 'preconditions of original sin', as well as that Faustian fascination with bad conscience.[6] As for the journey in prospect, there was some way to go before its nature could even be stated in these terms. Nevertheless, from the outset, assisting Regine in her present unhappy state would be one way of remaining faithful to her.

Kierkegaard's claim that he 'wrote *Either/Or* for her' can in this light mean more than that he wrote the 'The Seducer's Diary' that concludes Part One to 'repel her'.[7] The entire work can be seen as the start of a pilgrimage on which any willing reader can accompany Kierkegaard on the way to the kind of blessing that he tries to find for himself. The idea that the 'Diary' would repel her was one that occurred to him in that time of 'deception', which was before the defence of the dissertation. Even then, for so good an analyst of his own mental states, it was a simplistic strategy that Regine would easily see through. The better idea behind the ruse would be to ensure widespread sympathy for Regine in escaping marriage with such a scoundrel. People were indeed scandalized by the 'Diary'. Heiberg in reviewing *Either/Or* said that, although he could envisage a character like the seducer, he could never imagine an author who found pleasure in putting himself into such a character's shoes.[8]

By the time *Either/Or* was published, the deception would be unnecessary in any case; events would prove that it was the faithfulness that Kierkegaard harped on in the mind-tossed tumult of his cabin that took over the helm. Regine might in that connection pick up a quite different message more subtly inscribed on the text's surface, or if we prefer, on that vast and, to rightly focused eyes, instructive envelope in which the now less-relevant put-off was enclosed.

The first of the two long sections of Part Two of *Either/Or* is, to all appearances, a sustained argument for marriage as part of an ethical life-view. The pseudonymous author is a lower court judge, Assessor Wilhelm, who sees himself as having successfully 'realized the universal', this being the recurring formula in the early pseudonyms in connection with the goal of an ethically motivated life. The form of the book is evidently adversarial. The judge in Part Two of *Either/Or* presents arguments defending an ethical life-view against claims made for the benefits of a life of pleasure. Readers unsurprisingly find that the judge's high-minded exhortations and dry style compare unfavourably with the liveliness and expressive immediacy of his addressee's contributions in Part One of *Either/ Or*. The suspicion is that the real author is more at home with the aesthete than with the ethicist, but in the final pages of Part Two, at the end of the second of the judge's two long epistles, Regine would be able to read of the possibility of a 'noble' exception to the ideal of 'realizing the universal'.[9]

As advocated by Assessor Wilhelm, realizing the universal means having the civic as well as family responsibilities that support and perpetuate the state. If there are to be exceptions (and, as Kierkegaard would typically point out later, it is a failure of exceptionality on their part if *they* were to gang together), they must be those who would still prefer to realize the universal rather than, as with the aesthete, refuse to. They must be prevented by some circumstance that calls for them to sacrifice that ambition. The whole drift of the judge's case is directed not at this possibility, but at his young friend's willing failure to take advantage of the benefits of something he can choose. The benefits include the continuity and depth of a life in which the universal is realized, thus allowing the aesthete to form a socially visible 'self' out of the pieces of a more or less dissipated life. With regard to marriage, in comparing the opposed perspectives of an aesthetic and an ethical life-view, the judge says that ethical continuity enriches rather than impoverishes its aesthetic aspects and it adds to love a time dimension of which the aesthete's focus on the moment of pleasure cheats him. Subject to their own whims, and relying on outward circumstances for opportunities to satisfy them, exponents of an aesthetic life-view never 'make anything of themselves', to recall the phrase Michael Pedersen Kierkegaard used concerning his errant youngest son. A *noble* exception, however, is someone forced to *sacrifice* these benefits. A high price has to be paid for being the exception – even a 'purgatory'.[10]

*Either/Or* is an open-ended work of (in the new critical edition) 769 pages, and it concludes abruptly with a 'Last Word' (*Ultimatum*) in the form of a sermon (by a priest from Jutland, Kierkegaard's father's home base). The priest proclaims that 'before God we are always in the wrong'. The work thus ends with something that has yet to be said and which, when said, will suggest that even a decision in favour of the ethical will not suffice for human fulfilment. There is something radically wrong with the ethicist's grasp of what it is to realize the universal. It assumes – as the next but one work to appear was to put it – that 'the ethical is the universal and as such, in turn, the divine'.[11] What is left unsaid on all those pages, and waiting to be explained, is the idea that the universal seen as the proper aim of morality can be realized in some quite other way, perhaps through a relationship to an Archimedean point outside the universal possible only for exceptions – that is, for those forced to stand outside and able to take the strain.

While in Berlin Kierkegaard read copiously and kept up a correspondence not only with his friend Emil, but with colleagues, Sibbern and his two nieces and four nephews. Besides Schelling's lectures, he also attended others', though with limited enthusiasm. But it was Schelling's he had ostensibly come to Berlin to audit. Was it just an excuse to get away? It seems not. Indeed, Kierkegaard began with high hopes of learning something useful for his own development. The lectures were promoted as providing a corrective to the prevailing Hegelian philosophy.

In fact, Schelling had been called from Munich to Berlin by the authorities precisely to counteract the politically disruptive influence of the 'Left' Hegelians. Much was expected of Hegel's renegade former ally and fellow student. Those who came to hear him included a young Swiss and future famous historiographer of art and culture (Jakob Burckhardt), an aspiring social anarchist from Russia (Mikhail Bakunin) and Karl Marx's colleague Friedrich Engels, who, as an ardent Hegelian, had come to defend the interests of the master. All were younger contemporaries of Kierkegaard. What Kierkegaard himself might hope for can conveniently be phrased – even if all too summarily – in the terms of that individually accessed Archimedean point outside the world. To Hegel, the very idea would be symptomatic of a failure to grasp the nature of human involvement in the world. Properly understood, there is nothing 'outside' the universal, which in its ethical aspect is embodied in society as *it* develops. Reality is properly grasped in proportion to the way in which the world we live in is *itself* seen to provide the wherewithal for collective human fulfilment. Not that Hegel left no space for religion; in the world of change that makes up history, religion was, he said, 'the place where man is always assured of finding a consciousness of the unchangeable'.[12] Hegel, as can be guessed, was widely perceived as a pantheist for whom the personal God of religion dissolves into the developing world as we find it. The divine will is at work in the creation itself as it presently stands ('to reason', as one might add).

But Schelling saw things otherwise; for him, everything began in a kind of metaphysical Big Bang, a counterpart of original sin that left a diversity that needs gradually to come together with human help. Actually to help requires will and understanding, and for this, a source is found in a personal God, this deity being by no means a human invention, as in Feuerbach or Freud, but a contrivance of the world itself in providing an example to those who can properly assist in the process of unification. 'Personality' was a crucial concept. For Kierkegaard, because a personal God was integral to his inherited faith, it was clear that his antecedent sympathies lay with Schelling. Where, according to Schelling, Hegel's philosophy was in its entirety negative, through having confused a mere representation of the intellectual form in which God *would* reveal himself with his actually doing so, Schelling promised to deliver what many had heard rumours of – namely, a 'positive' philosophy that was to be his own version of the 'System', and which would reconcile faith with science, and philosophy with revelation. The extensive notes that Kierkegaard took from the lectures testify to the seriousness of his own hopes. To his intense disappointment – but as Engels no doubt had expected – Schelling was content to establish the fact and content of revelation through yet another Hegelian-style history, in this case that of religious experience, beginning with mythology and culminating in mysticism and theosophy. There was nothing here that could help the individual facing those contingencies that force decisions on those intent on a good life. Where Hegel had reduced God to the 'concept', all that his former colleague could offer was yet another set of abstractions without bearing on selfhood and existence. Towards the end of his Berlin stay, in a letter to Emil Boesen, Kierkegaard describes Schelling as 'talk[ing] endless nonsense both in an intensive and an extensive way'.[13]

It was not only Part One's 'Seducer's Diary' that had begun life before Kierkegaard's departure from Copenhagen. Several of the opening aphorisms (*diapsalmata*) in Part One attributed to the aesthete are early journal entries from as far back as the Faustian 1836. The greater appeal that readers tend to find in Part One is doubtless due not only to the infamous story of a seduction but to the more directly living origins of these aphoristic expressions of Romantic irony. Immediately after the pseudonymous editor's preface, we read, 'What is a poet? An unhappy man who hides deep anguish in his heart, but whose lips are so formed that when the sigh and the cry pass through them, it sounds like lovely music.'[14] It becomes clear in the long run that Kierkegaard saw the transition from Part One to Part Two of *Either/Or* as providing something essential that the aesthete lacks – ever more obviously so as Part One traces a spiritual descent from the innocence of unreflective and immediate pleasure to the cold and compulsively repetitive satisfactions of the successful seducer. What does the aesthete lack? He lacks a 'self'. If the noble exception must forgo the comforts of home life, the aesthete, spreadeagled time-wise in his serial dependency on what life has to offer, is not even at home to himself.

*Either/Or*'s readers would of course not have read the Gilleleje Testament. If they had done so, they would see here, now framed in the language of life-views, a huge and imaginative working out of the declaration's seminal thoughts on pleasure and ethics, the search for an 'I' and the need for a God that we can relate to only by rising above the 'externals' of our identities in time. What is new is the focus on marriage. Kierkegaard himself says that the reason why the second part of *Either/Or* begins with marriage is that it 'is the most profound form of the revelation of life'.[15] There is no qualification to the effect that this was just a view he attributed to Assessor Wilhelm. Perhaps, then, Kierkegaard genuinely considered this to be the profoundest form of the revelation of life – at least, ideally. Not realizing the universal in the judge's way would mean sacrificing this most profound way of revealing life.

In a late journal entry, however, Kierkegaard would write, 'what the judge says in his way . . . is what you would expect of a married man who champions marriage with ethical enthusiasm.'[16] Prefixing 'just' to 'what' would make the remark *openly* disparaging. Any enthusiasm that Kierkegaard himself might have felt for marriage at that later time would have to be religious rather than ethical in the judge's sense. As it was, in those later years Kierkegaard tended increasingly and problematically to see celibacy and the single state as a requirement of the true Christian.[17] Whether or not he would say that the true Christian reveals life in some yet deeper form, one in which the true Christian has to remain in some way unrevealed to others, the sacrifice is in any case just as great. In a 'Report to History' (*The Point of View for My Work as an Author*), published after his death, Kierkegaard claimed that he was deeply affected religiously when writing *Either/Or*. Having abandoned the 'soothing' idea of married life, but also turning his back on the life of 'despair and sensuality', he had retired to the 'cloister'. The name given to the work's editor is appropriately Victor Eremita (Triumphant Recluse).

In letters to his friend Emil Boesen, the would-be celibate hermit nevertheless constantly begged for news of Regine. Giving Boesen the days and times he would most likely catch her on the street, he even asked him to spy on her. With apparently the same end in view, he wrote to his nephews and nieces, just in case they had anything to tell. Someone had told him of Regine inviting some of them to her home. We may imagine a twofold concern: a genuine worry about her condition but also a personal interest in her attitude to him, since he also spoke of a 'return' but with its nature unspecified. With tongue conspicuously in cheek, and reckoning that Emil would understand the point, he also told him on *no* account to tell anyone about his having seen a delightful young opera singer who reminded him so much of Regine, and whose closer acquaintance he would have sought had he not been too busy: 'I have no time to get married.'[18] Emil, kept well informed of progress with *Either/Or*, was also sent to order a copy of Heiberg's translation of the French dramatist A. E. Scribe's vaudeville *First Love*, in this case with genuine orders to keep it quiet. A piece on that play was to be included in Part One of *Either/Or*.

That was in December 1841. Kierkegaard wrote at the beginning of February that he was impatient to return home and to his library.

Emil Boesen (1812–1881), Kierkegaard's life-long friend and only true confidant.

A month later, he disembarked at Copenhagen with the 'aesthetic' defence of marriage in his baggage and by the middle of April, finishing touches were made to the 'Diary'. He had begun preparing drafts of the latter from earlier notes in January. While in Berlin, he had also drafted his new 'take' on Antigone, 'Ancient Tragedy's Reflection in the Modern', in which the tragic heroine is given a 'reflection' that the Greeks were as yet unable to provide: a pain of solitude quite other than that of being about to be buried alive. The device for aesthetic sustainability, 'Crop Rotation', was also drafted there. The long essay on 'The Immediate Erotic Stages', to follow the tone-setting *diapsalmata* in Part One, was finished in June. In that essay, the 'stages' again follow the Hegel–Heiberg pattern and are illustrated by figures from three Mozart operas: the Page from *The Marriage of Figaro*, Papageno from *The Magic Flute* and the eponymous *Don Giovanni*. They represent, respectively, dreaming desire, searching desire and pure desire. By the end of July, Kierkegaard had completed the three portrayals of abandoned women (Shadowgraphs) for Part One and also (it is surmised) the short piece on 'The Unhappiest One', whose grave bears only that description.[19] The actual origin of the short essay on *First Love* is unclear, and the published text may be from an earlier review. The judge's second long epistle, 'Equilibrium between the Aesthetic and the Ethical', was ready in May. The concluding 'Last Word' had already been sketched, and the Preface was completed last of all in November 1842. Prefaces are, for obvious reasons, usually written last, but in this case there can be a reason besides the need to have the whole in mind before trying to introduce it. Kierkegaard wanted readers, too, to get an impression of the whole and not simply read the work *seriatim*, which of course was the way in which it would be read – at least by those who did not buy the book merely to read the 'Diary'. It seems as though Kierkegaard wanted to leave it to each reader – having taken sides, or unable to do so or like him gone further – to provide his or her own preface.

I called the work Either/Or and tried in the Preface to explain the meaning of this. After familiarizing myself with all the parts, I had let the whole thing come together in my mind in a moment of contemplation. My proposal was that the reader should do the same. For him too the whole thing was to be like a point, divided disjunctively. But here the reader would enter into a relation of self-activity with the book, as I had intended he should and had sought to bring this about by abstaining completely from saying anything about the plan of the work; in any case I was in no position to have any more definite view on this than any other reader, should there be one. The plan was a task for self-activity, and to impose my own understanding on the reader seemed to me an offensive and impertinent meddling. Every person experiences an either/or in his life . . . But the grasp of the plan will differ according to the degree of the individual's development.[20]

6

# The Shower Bath

The publication of *Either/Or* on 20 February 1843 caused a furore. Young liberals read it with relish, but the establishment was shocked. Reviewing the work just a week later, Heiberg called it a 'monster' and with heavy humour made sport with its title: 'Am I *either* to read it, *or* shall I refrain?' Of 'The Seducer's Diary' (having of necessity chosen the former option), he was in no doubt: 'one is disgusted, revolted, offended.'[1] A devoted nephew, Henrik Sigvard Lund, expressed the general excitement aroused by its publication. Writing to his other uncle, the naturalist Peter Wilhelm Lund in Brazil, he said he would send a copy of a book that has made a 'great stir and is read by nearly every cultivated person . . . its title is *Either/Or* and it is assumed that Søren is the author.'[2] Only assumed, because officially the real author was shielded from being directly addressed, or even properly named, as the author until admitted, as was done by Kierkegaard at the end of this period of writing in an addendum to *Concluding Unscientific Postscript*. At the time, however, Søren was maintaining a frivolous 'man about town' facade that might actually have tricked people into thinking he could not have been the author.

Kierkegaard, in other words, was now engaged in another deception. Earlier he had been employing his wit to banish the thought of his loss; but now he was using it to hide from others the energy that he had found, not just in a remarkable literary talent, but in the (heaven-sent?) opportunity provided by that very loss to indulge in that talent. His and Regine's sorry fate had given him a theme on which to test his skills further. About two months after the publication of *Either/Or*, Kierkegaard visited Berlin once again, but this time only for a short period. He arrived there on 6 May and in a letter to Emil Boesen all but three weeks later, wrote,

> I have finished a work of some importance to me, am hard at work on another, and my library is indispensable to me, as is also a printer. In the beginning I was ill, but now I am well, that is to say, insofar as my spirit grows within me and probably will kill my body. I have never worked as hard as now. I go for a brief walk in the morning. Then I come home and sit in my room without interruption until about three o'clock. My eyes can barely see. Then with my walking stick in hand I sneak off to the restaurant, but am so weak that I believe if anyone were to call out my name, I would keel over and die. Then I go home and begin again. In my indolence during the past months I had pumped up a veritable shower bath, and now I have pulled the string and the ideas are cascading down upon me: healthy, happy, merry, gay, blessed children born with ease and yet all of them with the birthmark of my personality . . .[3]

The healthy, blessed children found their place in an impressively diverse series of pseudonymous publications. A first version of one of these was fully drafted on Søren's arrival back to Copenhagen on 30 May 1843, but he also had sketches and a synopsis for another. The former was a strange hybrid of a work to be called *Repetition* and the second the one book that, when completed, Kierkegaard thought would make him world famous. It was *Fear and Trembling*. Although he returned with a full draft of the first version of *Repetition*, it seems evident that this other work was the one that he was still working on 'in full spate' and called for some checking in his library. Diversity in genre as well as in topic are reflected in the choices of pseudonym, but the topics all relate to Kierkegaard's personal dilemmas, and the works are easily read as attempts to grasp a way in which religion could help him in resolving them.

In its graphic way, *Fear and Trembling* pursues the topic of the noble exception introduced at the close of *Either/Or*. The book is an illustrated commentary on Abraham's willingness at God's command, and as proof of his faith, to sacrifice his only son Isaac. We ask why he should have chosen this extreme example of faith combined with evident cruelty. God seems here, at first glance, to be no better than a mafia boss demanding proof of loyalty in the grossest possible way. Informed by Kierkegaard's personal motives, a second glance can soften the picture.

Although some material from that time found its way, with necessary adjustments, into *Fear and Trembling*, a journal entry from that earlier time had asked – it seems merely speculatively – what the 'weightiest sacrifice that God could command' would be.[4] At that moment, Kierkegaard's focus was on Abraham's unqualified trust and his unwavering facing of God's command.[5] A passage in Kierkegaard's draft sermon carried over into *Fear and Trembling* goes, 'We ought [to] attend particularly to this trusting, God-devoted disposition, to this cheerful and unhesitating willingness to face trials, to answer bravely: Here I am.' It continues,

> Is it the same with us, or are we not, if anything, eager to evade the situation when we sense that difficult trials draw near, wishing for nothing so much an out-of-the-way corner of the world in which to hide ourselves, wishing that the mountains would conceal us?[6]

But now, reflecting on his own personal dilemma, Kierkegaard would be quite aware of the poignancy of a situation in which, instead of 'realizing the universal' in the socially transparent roles of priest and husband, he had retreated into the privacy of his own study to write *about* realizing the universal. This was not saying,

'Here I am.' There is another side. He was concealing this feverish activity by appearing in public in a role reminiscent of his own portrait of the aesthete. What greater contrast could there be than this between Abraham's transparent and unwavering trust and a deceptive recluse with too little faith to keep a promise? Crucially enough, the notes that Kierkegaard had made at the time of drafting that sermon include one under the heading 'God's Test', saying, 'God's tests are grounded in love.'[7] All who know the resolution of the Genesis story, in which God commands Abraham to stay his hand and provides a lamb for the sacrifice, may choose to see the story in that light. But for personal reasons, Kierkegaard's focus was on the test of faith. He was comparing himself unfavourably with an Abraham trudging up to the mountain steadfastly intent on killing his son to show his continued trust.

A journal entry predicting *Fear and Trembling*'s fame brings the personal dilemma in closer to its text. Kierkegaard notes that the 'deliberate mystification' he was spreading at the time was not so much that the writing was being done under cover as the fact that it 'reproduced' his own life.[8] The work's scene-setting 'Attunement' alludes to the woman blackening her breast to deceive the child when the time comes for it to be weaned. Kierkegaard was not only failing to present himself as himself; he was tricking Regine out of her attachment to him by pretending to be an unappealing villain. What greater contrast could there be to Abraham's unhesitating willingness to face his trial and answer bravely, 'Here I am'?

*Fear and Trembling* is easily taken, disturbingly, to reproduce Kierkegaard's life in another way. If it is Kierkegaard's sacrifice of Regine that reproduces Abraham's obedience to God, then Kierkegaard becomes a crazed man trying to keep in with a petulant deity. That description fits the Old Testament deity better than a God of love outside time, and it is the latter that Kierkegaard hints at in vindication of the noble exception. The relationship to God was still to be explained, to his readers and to himself, but when eventually brought to light, it turns out to be a matter of prayer and imitation rather than obedience. As it was at the time, there was certainly little in Kierkegaard's own conduct that could measure up to the unwavering faith with which Abraham strode off to the mountain intent on sacrificing his son.

In the end, *Fear and Trembling* leaves its reader little the wiser as to what to conclude from the fact that the father of faith turns out by conventional standards to be either plain mad or a murderer. Kierkegaard himself was obviously neither, just someone on whom one might look with disgust or pity for failing to conform with current conventions of human solidarity. *Fear and Trembling*'s success may be due as much to its suggestive obscurity as to the elegant conciseness and pregnancy of its prose.

The more mundane title of *Repetition* is due to a failed attempt by Kierkegaard literally to reproduce a part of his life. It was an everyday experience that put Kierkegaard in mind of another line of thought that led him into leaving *Fear and Trembling*.[9] There are no preliminary sketches for this new work, and the fact that Kierkegaard arrived home with a first version in full draft indicates a work written on impulse. What had struck him upon his return to Berlin and looking around was how not only had the familiar surroundings changed but so had his mood. He had written on arrival to Emil Boesen telling of the uneasy state he was in, although he was now once again 'afloat' and the 'machinery within [him] fully at work', and

as to my internal state in other respects, I will not say much, or rather nothing, for I will not tell lies. My address is Jägerstrasse und Charlottenstrasse an der Ecke, my old address, but the owner has married and therefore I am living like a hermit in one room, where even my bed stands. I do not want to bother speaking the German language, and therefore I live as isolated as possible.[10]

In the finished work, the narrator describes a fictitious return to Berlin as a failure to repeat – in the sense of reproduce – a previous visit:

> My home had become dismal to me precisely because it was the wrong kind of repetition. My thoughts were barren, my anxious imagination constantly conjured up tantalizing memories of how the thoughts had presented themselves the last time, and the weeds of these recollections strangled every other thought.[11]

The narrative is in the pen of one Constantin Constantius, a worldly man with psychological insight and the cool attitude with the touch of cynicism that often goes with that. It allows him to sympathize with a young man he meets by chance and who is in the throes of an unhappy love affair. His inherent concern with others, being typically that of an observer, Constantin's interest in the younger man is initially a form of aesthetic fascination. This proves to be an advantage since it enables him to uncover his young friend's deeper motives. These are to be found in what Constantin describes as a state of spiritual puberty, where things are not yet under a control that comes with age and experience. The young man is engaged to a girl with whom he professes to be deeply in love, but to whom he also feels he owes something. Constantin sees immediately that the 'girl's charms' are not the main thing; it is his 'regret over having wronged her by disturbing her life' that upsets the young man.[12] The latter blames his melancholy for his lack of resolution, but Constantin perceives that his new friend is really through with the relationship. She is, or rather she herself now was, 'the occasion that awakened the poetic in him'.

Anyone knowing details of Kierkegaard's year-long engagement would see straight away the biographical implications of the tale unfolding in *Repetition*. But at the time the *auto*biographies of the two involved were their private affairs. In all likelihood, Regine would alone see the reality behind a literary prism that turns a would-be scoundrel into a cynical conspirator able to suggest that the young man set up another girl in an apartment with doors onto two streets, so that no one need know how short a time he actually spends there. After first approving of the plan, the young man then finds he cannot go through with it and leaves town. Constantin never sees him again. The work ends with a letter to 'my dear reader' addressed as 'Mr X Esq.', to which is enigmatically added 'the real reader of this book'. The opening lines are

> Forgive me for speaking confidentially to you, but we are *unter uns* [only the two of us]. Despite the fact that you are an imaginary person, you are in no way a multiplicity, but only one, so there is only you and I.[13]

Kierkegaard, two days prior to departure for Berlin, had, under his own name, published two of what were to be a series of 'edifying discourses'. They were dedicated to 'Michael Pedersen Kierkegaard, formerly hosier here in the city', and sought out 'that individual' whom 'with joy and gratitude' Kierkegaard could call 'his' reader'. The poetic intensity and high seriousness of these discourses indicate a dedication to the 'part' of his father's religion. But he may also have been showing to his dead father that he could shine in this area too – or was it to redress the balance in favour of a more faithful picture of his own relation to life than that conveyed by presumed authorship of *Either/Or*, to say nothing of its infamous 'Diary'? All six sets of, in all, eighteen discourses are preceded by prefaces expressing in subtle and almost self-deprecatory language the hope that they may find their way to '*my* reader, that single individual'. The first preface is dated 5 May 1845. That was Kierkegaard's thirtieth birthday. In a summative journal entry from 1849, he notes how what had concerned him personally 'form[ed] into something with wide application': 'the individual' was something he had understood 'from very early on', but

> when I first wrote I was thinking of my reader in particular, for that book [the two edifying discourses published in May 1843] contained a little hint to her, and then for the time being it was especially true for me that I only sought that one single reader.[14]

Much later he wrote – in a nomination it would be hard to believe had only a retrospective effect – that the preface was intended for Regine. It was to her that the discourse 'stretches out its arms' – to 'that single individual who is favourably enough disposed to allow him [or her]self to be found'.[15]

That Regine read the book appears from a conversation Kierkegaard had with Sibbern – a fact he had learned from Regine herself.[16] All during the previous year, Kierkegaard had been avoiding the person who was now his secret addressee. The reason was fear that she would misinterpret his unexpectedly early return from Berlin, thinking it a sign that she had been on his mind all along. Three weeks before his departure on the second visit, Kierkegaard was led to believe that she knew all along that he was not a scoundrel: at evensong on Easter Sunday, 16 April 1843, after the sermon, Regine had turned in his direction and nodded twice.

> I do not know if it was pleadingly or forgivingly but in any case so affectionately, I had taken a seat at a remote spot but she spotted me. Would to God she hadn't. Now a year and a half of suffering are wasted and all the enormous pains I took; she does not believe I am a deceiver, she trusts me.[17]

Afterwards, 'knowing the road I usually take', Regine made a point of having their paths cross every Monday between nine and ten in the morning. A page has been torn out of the journal at this point, but the same entry goes on to say that although he has done everything to shield her from any sense of guilt for what happened, and has kept his own reactions to himself, by failing to take his melancholy seriously and by provoking his pride, she has made matters worse for them both.

In setting out for Berlin with *Fear and Trembling* as his main preoccupation, Kierkegaard must also have been thinking of how to repair what he saw as this new breach. If she couldn't be repelled, at least he could try to explain himself, and that might also help her. Who knows? Maybe there could be some kind of reunion. When the thought of repetition had occurred to him in Berlin, Kierkegaard was no longer thinking of the break-up as having to be explained away; it might be an opportunity for renewal at some higher level. He had shown with *Either/Or* behind him that he could 'make something' of himself on his own. But he had also shown to himself how he would explain to her and to himself the kind of humanly insoluble dilemmas that arise when the everyday and religion come in conflict, as he had come to believe they must. If they both had faith, then the unhappy events could in the end acquire for each of them a 'repetition', even if in the very nature of repetition, its outcome was not clear. He could also give his version of how the unhappiness came about and of his own part in it, including the deception. In words that have to us, if less immediately to Kierkegaard's contemporaries, an unmistakably author-biographical ring, he has Constantin Constantius offer his young friend the following diagnosis of his ills:

> He was deeply and passionately in love, this was clear, and yet he was already, in the earliest days, in a position to recollect his love. He was basically finished with the whole relationship . . . And yet she was the beloved, the only one he had ever loved, the only one he would ever love . . . All this was accompanied by a strange change in him. A poetic productivity awakened

in him, to an extent that I would not have thought possible. Now I understood everything. The young girl was not his beloved, she was simply the cause that awakened the poetic in him and thus transformed him into a poet. This was why he could love only her, never forget her, never wish to love anyone else, and yet still merely long for her. She had permeated every aspect of his being. She had made him into a poet, and with this signed her own death-sentence.[18]

Eight letters from the young man to his 'silent confidant' form much of the second part of *Repetition*. Constantin receives but cannot answer them, since the young man has left no address. Oddly for the reader, in a letter concluding the work, we read that this young man is really Constantin's fabrication. The invented young man also talks of repetition but in a more heated way. In comparing his own suffering to that of Job – who, like Abraham, sided with faith but lost everything, whereas Isaac, in the end, was saved – he says, 'Job is blessed and has got everything *double* – this is called a *repetition*.'[19] The thought of some form of shared identity with one who suffers on a cosmic scale no doubt gives some comfort at the prospect of recovery. But then Job's repetition is in a sense immaculate. He has done no wrong. In ordinary life, where in the face of God we are always in the wrong, our repetitions must take guilt into account. But Constantin Constantius's advisory brief extends only to sketching a framework that allows for a 'religious' exception. As an ironist, he is incapable of adopting it himself. In the capacity of 'a midwife in relation to the child she has delivered', he therefore *leaves* us with the young man. Once the delivery is over, Constantin, like the midwife and in his own words, 'pale[s] into insignificance'.[20] He steps discreetly aside to leave the reader (and the writer too) to wrestle with a repetition that offers exoneration and is unavailable to a merely 'poetic' exception.[21]

This published conclusion was not the one Kierkegaard had brought with him from Berlin. The original version has the young man commit suicide, leaving both Constantius and his young friend out of the way. Given the circumstances, that ending was hardly a concealed threat that Kierkegaard might do the same. The idea could be that repetition is an impossible ideal for creatures that remain earthbound; but since, unlike the ironical Constantius, Kierkegaard himself was on the threshold of a religious perspective, there was still a possibility of a form of religious repetition here on earth. A journal entry from the time says that faith 'has hopes for this life, but, be it noted, on the strength of the absurd, not by virtue of human understanding', for otherwise it is 'only good sense, not faith'.[22] What form might such a repetition take? Could it be the 'erotica[lly] utopian' hope Garff suggests? It is a hope

> of being able to resume the relationship with Regine in a more platonic form to be realized within Copenhagen's ramparts, which like a kind of monastery wall could encircle their chaste meetings, making them the modern age's answer to the monk and the nun.[23]

Perhaps it could be, but the needle of Kierkegaard's volatile imagination may have flickered between this and other variations on a scale whose lowest reading could be that Regine simply appreciated or perhaps even learned from his having this utopian thought.

It was sometime in July after his return from that second Berlin visit that Kierkegaard learned of Regine's engagement to Johan Frederik (Fritz) Schlegel. The news must have stopped him in his tracks. Her former house tutor, Schlegel was a personable and conscientious man with whom she had been on promisingly friendly terms before Kierkegaard burst in on the scene to upstage him. All variations on a scale of more or less erotic repetition were

Johan Frederik ('Fritz') Schlegel (1817–1896), lawyer and civil servant and Regine's former house tutor, whom she married in 1843. From 1855 until 1861 he was Governor General of the Danish West Indies and later Mayor of Copenhagen.

now out of the question. It seems, ironically as Garff observes, that the only repetition left on the table was Regine's more mundane reunion with Fritz.

As for *Repetition*'s real author, through a bitterness and disappointment sarcastically expressed in his journal by suggesting that the 'kindness' she had shown him might be paid off by cash, he had to set about bringing the young man back to life.²⁴ The last of the eight letters to Constantin Constantius, now forming much of the second part, reports,

> She is married, to whom I do not know, because when I read it in the newspaper I felt as if I had been struck and I dropped the paper . . . Since then I have not been able to bring myself to take a closer look at the announcement.²⁵

Recalling those two nods in the Church of Our Lady at evensong, Kierkegaard was now forced to reinterpret the episode and the subsequent crossings of their paths. Far from being an expression of forgiveness and understanding, it had been a request for his approval of the betrothal. Her subsequent friendliness was because she thought she had received it.

Regine's new engagement must nevertheless have left Kierkegaard free now to put aside much of the guilt he still felt at the break; he could let his thoughts dwell on wider aspects of the dilemmas into which it had brought him. In writing to Emil Boesen on arrival that second time in Berlin, and announcing the completion of a work 'of some importance' to him, he had said,

> wherever I end up, I shall never forget to employ the passion of irony in its justified defiance of any non-human half-philosophers who understand neither this nor that, and whose whole skill consists in scribbling down German compendia and thus defiling what has a worthier origin by making nonsense of it.[26]

In 1844, aside from giving the trial sermon required for admission into the state church, Kierkegaard published all of six books. In March, June and August, there were three new sets of discourses, while June saw what in theme if not style is, in academic terms, the most philosophical of his works: *Philosophical Crumbs* (also translated as *Fragments*). Its pseudonymous author Johannes Climacus was one that Kierkegaard had used earlier in the unpublished 'Johannes Climacus eller De omnibus dubitandum est [Johannes Climacus or Everything Is to Be Doubted]'. The pseudonym here is close to being Kierkegaard's clone, a student trying his hand at a 'little speculation', as Kierkegaard himself put it later – that is to say, some philoso-phizing in the Hegel style.[27] It took the form of a story of a young student whose ambition it was to reach an eternal consciousness by way of thinking. The historical Johannes Climacus was a seventh-century monk and saint who spent many years by Mount Sinai and wrote a work called *Scala paradisi* (Ladder of Divine Ascent). Its conclusion is an anticipation of *Repetition*'s theme that there is no meeting of 'ideal' and 'actual' either in time or in eternity, but only in consciousness.

In this published work, Johannes Climacus is less the real Kierkegaard in disguise than a fictional author whose own consciousness is on the level of a 'humorist', a notch higher than Constantin Constantius' irony. The latter may be seen as paving the way to the need for the religious framework, but the humorist actually grasps that framework with its implications and requirements. 'Edited' by Kierkegaard, the humorist offers in spare language an alternative to a philosophical epistemology based on that which Plato attributes to Socrates, namely that eternal truth is found in recollection. Although of ancient origin, the idea is one that in its various forms has pervaded traditional philosophizing since, not least that of the 'half-philosophers' at whom Kierkegaard said he would direct the 'passion' of his irony. As a famous quotation from the journals puts it, 'life is understood backwards but has to be lived forwards.'[28] The 'working' question of the *Crumbs* is whether and how an 'eternal happiness' can be made to depend on something past, a fact of history – namely, the Incarnation. In its original version, the question was posed more personally in the form 'how can *I* build *my* eternal consciousness on a piece of historical knowledge?'[29] The work was indeed originally drafted under Kierkegaard's own name and with the provisional title 'Philosophical Pieces – or a Small Bit of Philosophy'. That the alleged knowledge in question is the Christian Incarnation is made explicit only later in the work's extensive 'Postscript'.

But now there appeared, in the very same month, *The Concept of Anxiety: A Simple Psychologically Oriented Deliberation in View of the Dogmatic Problem of Hereditary Sin*, its author Vigilius Haufniensis

(Watchful Citizen of Copenhagen). The argument here is that, far from Adam being the sole originator of sin, we are all in Adam's position and lose our innocence similarly – except, of course, that in the meantime a whole culture of sin has developed to form an entrenched background to all our lives. As we become aware of the distinction in ourselves between 'I' and 'me', we are exposed to, and habituated to adopting, de-spiritualizing roles that allow us to merge again safely with the world. Haufniensis's message is that the anxieties we give in to, and which are fashionably treated 'with powder and with pills' should be grasped as our sole opportunity for spiritual growth: 'Whoever has learned to be anxious in the right way has learned the ultimate.'[30]

Although in both of these works Kierkegaard is no longer focused on his own personal dilemmas, the engagement and Regine still creep in when the occasion offers. In *Crumbs*, a passage describing a king falling unhappily in love with a peasant girl illustrates a 'type of unhappy love' in which the unhappiness 'does not lie in the fact that the lovers cannot be united, but in that they cannot understand each other'.[31] The book might itself be taken as living proof of the reason why, even in the passion of his irony, Kierkegaard thought too much and Regine was too passionate.

As for *Anxiety*, some commentary has linked the very choice of the Garden of Eden scenario to the broken engagement. Haufniensis admits he can find no place for the serpent, since it turns up so unexpectedly, quite 'out of the green', as it were. Similarly, the circumstances of seduction are found unexpectedly and everywhere. *Anxiety* speaks of the serpent as enticing the woman so that it was only after she had been seduced that she seduced Adam in turn. A passage in the 'Seducer's Diary' had described how the young woman, on coming to the point of feeling that an engagement was 'too confining', then herself 'bec[ame] the tempter who seduce[d] me into going beyond the boundary of the normal'.[32] Perhaps Kierkegaard is saying indirectly that it was not he who seduced

Regine, but Regine who seduced him. The circumstances that Johannes the Seducer sneakily brings about are there in ordinary life and may occur anywhere and at any time, and it is they that are represented by the serpent.[33]

Yet a third work appeared in that June of 1844. It was *Prefaces: Light Reading for Different Conditions of People According to Time and Opportunity*, and the author was Nicolaus Notabene (Nicholas Notewell). It is a compilation of either unpublished or later revised prefaces that in a later reworking had Heiberg as their common but unnamed target. Kierkegaard had been provoked by a long article in which, in passing, Heiberg had criticized the author of *Repetition* for not distinguishing between repetitions in nature and those in the social world. As was the case with his remarks on Heiberg's criticism of *Either/Or*, the turns of phrase Kierkegaard used in a projected response were not of the kind that could appear in print. The published prefaces combine malice with glee and, of course, wit. Their own preface is almost as long as each of the two that it prefaces. And what is its topic? Prefaces, naturally. As an appropriate illustration of the genre, we are given an explanation of its own publication. It was a writer's compromise designed to ease Notabene's marriage or even save it. Adept enough in the noble art of thought to be able 'to dispute with the devil' (perhaps a reference to his brother), at home Notabene can never get beyond the preface, since every time he says something with which his wife disagrees, she exclaims affectionately but categorically 'you are just teasing me'. She tells him that for a married man to be an author is to be 'unfaithful'.[34] The comfortably married Nikolaus chooses to publish only prefaces.

For a year Kierkegaard had been occupied with the upbringing of those 'blessed children' that had descended on him. The occupation obviously energized him, but how far did it take him on that inland journey he had promised to his uncle in Brazil? How far had he come on the way from 'consciousness' to the 'preconditions of original sin'? The answer depends on how we interpret that phrase. With its focus on Adam, *The Concept of Anxiety* had at least taken him as a *writer* further in that direction. But we may choose to see progress here in the accompanying descant of edifying discourses published under Kierkegaard's own name. They at least testified to his continuing dedication to the God of his father. But if we understand by 'preconditions' the conceptual basis of the *idea* of original sin, then the measure of progress is found in the pseudonyms as they increasingly lay bare the nature of the choices before us in the context in which they have actually to be made – that is, not in thought but in action. In two years' time Kierkegaard would be 33, an age that he superstitiously connected with the deaths of his two sisters. Time might be running out. Two more works still to be wrought by his hyperactive imagination would bring closure and possibly even peace while still on earth.

For relaxation during this intense activity Kierkegaard would take frequent carriage rides into the countryside. It may be easier to imagine the peripatetic Kierkegaard more comfortably at home in a metropolis than in the calm of undisturbed nature. In between his peripatetic outings and tea shop conversations, we see him bending over his desk doing irreparable damage to his physique and rounding his shoulders. Yet this is someone who could say that 'the most agreeable, the most refreshing conversation is still that which is carried on by the trees'.[35] Copenhagen was a smallish city contained at the time by its ramparts, so it was easy to reach more peaceful surroundings, for instance Frederiksborg Gardens and also Assistens Graveyard, where his father was buried.[36] The pseudonymous works include many a walk in the wooded countryside, and Kierkegaard's own appreciation of landscapes and woodlands was already evident from his detailed descriptions of several long hikes during that summer recuperation at Gilleleje in 1835. The city streets allowed him to clear his mind for the next sentence or paragraph: 'Most of what I have written was spoken aloud many, many times, and often heard perhaps a score of times before being written down.'[37] But he would often venture through the portals of the ramparts and had once scorned the 'petit bourgeois' for never having felt 'nostalgia for some unknown, some remote something, never the profundity of being nothing at all, of strolling out of Nørreport with four shillings in your pocket and a slender cane in hand'. That, as we can guess, had been in the Faustian period, when the same narrow-minded citizens had 'no inkling' of a life-view in which the world was to be known 'through sin' and found on the other side of 'that dark realm of sighs, where one sees the crushed victims of seduction and enticement and the coldness of the tempter'.[38]

With his open hand writing undisputed religion and the other, still clenched, struggling to establish an active faith able to overcome the hindrances to a spiritual destiny, Kierkegaard's own actual and now-frequent carriage rides outside the gates were purely recreational. Sometimes with a friend, he would visit the woods north of Copenhagen and one or other of his favourite hostelries, in particular the coaching inn at Hørsholm, where he could spend the whole day eating well and talking with locals, who would be uninterested in the Copenhagen gossip. The excursions began in January, a time of feverish activity on Kierkegaard's part, and they continued through the year. Initially, the trips marked the ends of projects, but now he was struggling with the first part of a new work, and the carriage rides tended to coincide with periods of frustration. The text was 'In Vino Veritas', and it was planned as the first of two parts of a single volume entitled 'The Wrong and the Right'. Kierkegaard was now focusing on the problem of how to evaluate a life, one's own, and the topic was 'recollection'. What we call 'memory' is simply not forgetting; it has no more personal a meaning than 'turning a dog-ear in a book in order to remember where one left off'. But then there is also 'recollection', or remembering ourselves in situations of conflict in some or other mood and which can have caused regret. It is neither impersonal nor to be shared: the 'wine press of recollection everyone must tread alone'.[39] Under the pseudonym William Afham (William By-Him), 'In Vino Veritas' became the first of three 'studies by various persons' compiled by 'Hilarius Bogbinder' (Hilary Bookbinder) as *Stages on Life's Way*. A work of well over four hundred pages, the 'studies' include 'Some Reflections on Marriage in Answer to Objections' by 'A Married Man' and a new 280-page either/or: '"Guilty?" – "Not-Guilty?"'. The latter is subtitled 'A Story of Suffering, Psychological Experiment' and its author is Frater Taciturnus (Brother Silent). The book concludes with a letter to 'my dear reader' who, out of habit, we now identify as Regine, but in this case without the real author's authority. The writer goes on to say that, having come this far, there may be no readers left. Naturally only those who have stayed the course will be able to puzzle on the author's reason for saying this, and the remark can be compared with the ending of the next and even larger pseudonymous work, whose author ends by 'revoking' it – although only to the knowledge and surprise of a reader who has come far enough to stumble on that strange turn.

*Stages* is seen to be a re-working of *Either/Or* in the light of *Repetition* and *Fear and Trembling*. To read 'In Vino Veritas' is much like listening to a recording of a symposium (in the proper sense of a drinking party) with speeches by a series of spokesmen representing distinct but generally 'wrong' views about women. The participants include previous pseudonyms with modified backgrounds and attitudes. Victor Eremita has realized that the monastery is not the place from which to resist threats against spirituality: it is 'safer' to remain a recluse on the outside 'even if he travels all day and night in an omnibus'.[40] The 'married man', a younger version of Assessor Wilhelm, has as his motto 'the deceived are more wise than the deceiver' and thereby betrays a less stiff personality. He too addresses 'my dear reader', and the addressee that 'he' has in mind is clear enough. The theme is, again, 'the exception'. Wilhelm warns against intellectualized forms of religion that disparage the merely physical side of life, but he also cautions against revivalist religion. For the true religious exception, 'something must happen' and it must do so in the context of genuine love.[41] If not parading Kierkegaard's own problem, the author here is at least reverting to the kind of situation it exemplifies. In raising again the question of exceptionality and its justification, it is in the form of yet another either/or. If the order of composition may reasonably indicate an author's priorities, the question of exceptionality would seem here to be uppermost in Kierkegaard's mind. It was, after all, *his* problem, and he was even inclined to see it as *the* problem of the pseudonymous authorship.

Four years later, he would give the single individual a more 'public' meaning, even a political aspect, and he was able to say then that 'the pseudonyms, as books, also put the notion of the single individual into effect in relation to the reading public'.[42] But now in 1844, still in the midst of the pseudonyms, it is very probable that Kierkegaard was still trying to explain to himself as well as Regine – and anyone else whom their relationship concerned – how he might justify being an unmarried writer of books defending marriage instead of a hen-pecked married preface-monger like Notabene. He had already begun sketching *Stages* while in Berlin, where he had written to himself,

> Had I had faith I would have stayed with Regine. Praise be to God, I have now understood it. I have been on the point of losing my mind these days. [Humanly] speaking I have done the right thing for her, but perhaps I should never have become engaged.[43]

Appropriately enough the sketches were for what would be the work's central part: '"Guilty?" – "Not-Guilty?"'

As its real author feared, *Stages* received little notice when it appeared on 30 April 1845, and it sold badly. More contrived and less immediately accessible than its predecessors, all of them were still in the shadow of *Either/Or*. Kierkegaard tried not to mind: 'That's fine,' he wrote in the privacy of his journals, 'that way I'm quit the gawking rabble that wants to be on hand wherever it thinks something's astir.' When the silence continued, he began to think otherwise. Frustration and disappointment at the poor reception of this attempt to replace the original 'either/or' would be felt when Kierkegaard tried to drum up interest in these latest pseudonyms eight months later. Meanwhile, in May he paid another short visit to Berlin.

# 7

# Winding Up

True to form, simultaneously with *Stages*, Kierkegaard had with his open hand published *Three Discourses for Imagined Occasions*. The occasions were a communion, a marriage ceremony (appropriately enough) and at the graveside. These discourses continued that high-toned and, in their way, genuinely musical descant under which the pseudonyms had, for the last four years, been ringing out their upwardly striving improvisations. Soon more discourses would follow, but some important pseudonymous work was still to be done.

This work was undertaken in a sprawling and, at first glance, disorganized discursive ramble entitled *Concluding Unscientific Postscript to the Philosophical Crumbs*. The work's subtitle 'A Mimical, Pathetic-dialectic Compilation, an Existential Contribution' can be roughly rendered 'Miming of the interplay in real life of passion and a grasp of matters affecting our existence'. Paradoxically and contrary to its normal sense, the 'miming' is in the words for something that cannot be said. The 'blessed children' from that second Berlin visit are still to be heard but are not seen. The works in which they appeared are assigned to history as 'A Contemporary Effort in Danish Literature'. That effort is reviewed in an appendix to a subsection ('The Subjective Truth, Inwardness, Truth is Subjectivity'), in which they are exposed to the critical eye of Johannes Climacus, who, one of their number, in his official role as 'humorist', is also the *Postscript*'s author. He observes that his *Crumbs* had 'approached the problem of Christianity in a decisive way but without mentioning it by name or that of Christ'.[1] The name is now given and the general question posed: 'How to become a Christian.' No longer focused on bringing to light dilemmas to which the contingencies of life give rise, the *Postscript* opts for one horn of a dilemma and poses the question of how to grasp it.

The serried layers of two very unequal parts, chapters, sections, subsections and minor headings suggest a labyrinth in which it is all too easy to lose one's way. The structure is, however, quite simple. The first part briefly disposes of ways in which one cannot become a Christian just by retracing history, not even if the words of Christ have survived intact through the lapse of time. Nor can we become Christians by transposing Christianity into metaphysics – that is to say, through objective reasoning. Part Two has two main sections: one setting up the question of how to relate to Christianity once the task is seen as subjective, and a vastly longer second section devoted to what must be true of 'subjectivity' for the task to be properly presented and addressed in that way.

Why then is this task left in the hands of a self-styled humorist? The work is indeed full of humour as well as of satire and irony, but far from consistently so. Indeed, much of the detail shows no humour at all, and long passages repeatedly hammer the same point home. There are frequent footnotes in a style one could only treat as humour if the whole work were considered a joke, a satire, as early commentators tended to suggest. Climacus, however, provides his own 'theory' of humour, and it would be sophistical to take that too to be intended as a joke.

That theory presents humour as the proper stage prior to faith, a stage in which the demands of Christianity are clear but faith is not yet enacted. The task of the humorist is to 'make legitimate use of the comic against presumptuous forms of the religious'.[2] While irony looks down from a position that it likes to think is immune from its own ironic gaze, humour looks up at what it would have to accept even when, from a rational point of view, it is absurd. The 'ladder' implicit in Climacus' name is one on which the author stands, as it were, on the next highest rung. His virtue for the reader is his not having reached the highest, because once there, he would disappear from view and be practising that 'absolutely isolated humour that subsists in the person alone'. The reason for practising humour on his own would be that he knows that from a mundane point of view, the Christianity he practises *is* absurd. An example of this humour would be being able to say 'Thou' to God. One does so in 'the infinite pathos of religiousness', but it is 'infinitely comical' when you then turn around and repeat this personal form of address to the deity as you look back on the finite world and its uses of the vocative form. In Wittgensteinian terms, it would be a comical confusion of 'language-games' or an 'infinitely' colossal pun. In having to keep the language-games 'passionately' apart, a subjective thinker must be 'bifrontal'.[3]

The work's presentation of itself as 'unscientific' is also to be seen in this light. Kierkegaard's working title up to the final draft had been 'Concluding Simple-minded (*eenfoldig*) Postscript'. Since his own ideal of faith was of the simple kind that he had respected in his own father, the whole gist of the pseudonymous works, now apparent in the *Postscript*, was the disabusing of the less simple-minded of the superfluous knowledge on which they made their faith depend but which, in fact, only got in its way. However, Kierkegaard must have realized that in spite of being written with the faith of the more simple-minded in view, the work was not for *them*. He was really on their side. It is worth noting that it was among the 'ordinary' people that he had sought sanctuary in the streets from the oppressive atmosphere in his home. Among these, he no doubt tried himself to be as ordinary as he would have liked, unlike those who had contributed to the unnecessary clutter that got in the way of their faith. They were to be disabused of their notion that the saving truth was to be found down the path of scholarship and learning. For them, it was a convenient path. It offered a useful delay during which they could claim a kind of ancillary faith in the fact – so they liked to assume – that in treading it they were on their way to faith.

In *Postscript*, Kierkegaard's earthly targets are not lost to view. Nor are his earthly heroes. Poul Møller is there and also the German anti-Enlightenment thinkers Johann Georg Hamann and Friedrich Heinrich Jacobi, each on his path towards subjectivity. However, since the omnivorous Hegelian 'system' had engulfed them so that they were now no more than 'paragraphs' within it, they could be of little assistance, unlike the great literary critic and writer Gotthold Ephraim Lessing, whose agile ability to think subjectively happily enabled him to escape Hegel's clutches. Climacus elaborately praises Lessing but is careful not to cite him as an authority; Lessing as an authentically subjective thinker would have to decline any gesture of support or suggestion that he could give it. We also meet Johannes Climacus' greatest hero, Socrates, while among the targets are Martensen but also Mynster, an ally up to now but becoming less so. Heiberg comes in for some abuse for his repeated references to 'the demands of the times', as if these were something the times themselves could determine. In a short section of Part One, Grundtvig's plan for revitalizing the Danish Church – his 'matchless discovery' of substituting 'the living word' for ritual observance based on texts deciphered by intellectuals – is quickly dismissed as logically inconsistent.

As though to confirm that this 'concluding' postscript was literally bringing things to a close, Kierkegaard signs off as himself, but not before declaring his responsibility for all the pseudonyms. We learn from elsewhere that he did so only at the last minute and had long been 'in two minds' about such an acknowledgement. The causes for his indecision were external:

The lies and gossip and vulgarity that surround one make one's position fairly difficult at times, perhaps make me too anxious about having every last shred of truth on my side . . .[4]

Once made, this declaration could hardly come as a surprise. What *would* surprise, or more likely shock, any readers who had worked their way through more than five hundred pages would be to learn from Johannes Climacus, at that point, that everything he had said until then was to be 'understood in such a way that it is to be revoked'.[5]

Was this a final joke? Few nowadays see any basis for reading the humour in *Postscript* in this simplistic way, but one of the more influential proponents of such a view has pointed to what a plausible explanation might be:

> *Postscript* is a funny book with [the] frighteningly sober purpose . . . of [leading] its reader down a broad and prodigal path of merriment to the brink of the bottomless pit of freedom, [then] to surprise him with the absolute responsibility he bears for his own life.[6]

The motto attached to *Crumbs,* derived from Shakespeare's *Twelfth Night* in a German translation, may also help: 'Better Well Hanged than Ill Wed.' Better left unread than understood as a contribution to 'speculative' philosophy. A follow-up in *Postscript*'s preface offers a nice example of the ironic style of its frame. Johannes Climacus opens by saying his hopes that *Crumbs* should not be 'brought into affinity with the whole world' were more than fulfilled by it not being noticed at all. The author was left 'hanging' without anyone asking for whom. But that was just as well in a world too ready to impose its panegyrics on an author who tries to escape that kind of notice.

It is always awkward, even for the most insignificant traveller, to arrive at a town just when, in a state of the highest but most diverse expectation – some with cannons drawn up and fuses lit, with fireworks and illuminated placards in readiness, some with the town hall ceremoniously decorated, reception committee booted, speakers prepared, some with urgent systematic pen dripping and notebook opened – everyone is awaiting the arrival incognito of the promised one. A mistake can always happen. Literary mistakes of this kind belong to the order of the day.[7]

The literary mistake is easily identified. The dripping systematic pens hovering over open notebooks would straight away make subjective thinking into a topic of objective understanding. But as the first chapter of the first section of Part Two, devoted to subjectivity, makes clear, 'subjective' means subjective. If as a subjective thinker you think you have found a kindred spirit and then try calling him brother, you have still not understood. The quandary unfolds in a metaphor employing what must be one of the longest sentences in literature.

If a wretched amateur thinker, a speculative crank who, like a poor lodger, occupied an attic at the top of a vast building, sat there in his little closet, absorbed in what seemed to him difficult thoughts; if he began to conceive a dim suspicion that somewhere or other there must be something wrong with the foundations, without finding out more specifically how; if, whenever he looked out of his garret window, he shuddered as he saw the redoubled and hurried efforts to beautify or expand the building, so that after having seen and shuddered he subsided, drained of energy, uncomfortable as a spider who in its narrow nook sustains a miserable existence since the last house cleaning, all the while anxiously sensing a storm in the air; if, whenever he expressed his doubts to someone, he perceived that his speech, because of its departure from the usual manner of dressing up a thought, was regarded as the worn-out and bizarre costume of some unfortunate derelict – if, I say, such an amateur thinker and speculative crank were suddenly to make the acquaintance of a man whose celebrity did not directly ensure for him the validity of his thoughts (for the poor lodger was not quite so objective as to be able with no further ado to draw the conclusion backwards from renown to truth), but whose fame was for him, in his abandonment, nevertheless a smile of fortune, finding one or two of his difficult thoughts touched upon by the famous man: ah, what gladness, what festivity in the little garret chamber when the poor lodger took comfort in the glorious remembrance of the celebrity, while his occupation with thoughts took on confidence, the difficulties took on shape, and he the hope of understanding himself; i.e., the hope first of understanding the difficulty and then perhaps of being able to overcome it![8]

This is the author's introduction to the celebrity now to be introduced and lavishly praised in the following chapter. It is the aforementioned Lessing, whose contributions as a kindred spirit are outlined in the second and last chapter of this introductory section. The first chapter closes with a characteristic warning not to expect a genuinely subjective thinker to thank you when you tell him what you owe to him. If you 'parroted' to Lessing the ideas you had got from him and folded him admiringly in your arms, he would 'smilingly disengage himself' leaving you 'looking a fool'. If, on the other hand, you were to relate these thoughts to Lessing as if they were your own, he would 'thump me on the shoulder and say, with a look of ambivalent admiration, how right you are, if only I'd known'. Then 'I', concludes Johannes Climacus, 'if no one else, would understand that he had the better of me.'[9]

The implication is that any mere form of words about subjective thinking that two people would agree to cannot have subjective thinking as their topic. The claim will appear paradoxical in a work that puts words to that topic for well over four hundred more pages. However, what is really implied emerges when, well on into those pages, the author writes of an 'absolute orientation towards the absolute *telos* [goal]'. This is really just a new way of putting the Gilleleje declaration's idea of a unifying Archimedean point outside time. It is connected here with 'pathos', a state of mind that we acquire when we cease fudging distinctions and see what the options are. As the author points out, 'Pathos does not mean words; it means, for the one who exists, the transformation by this conception of the whole of his existence.'[10] It is the pathos of a need to relate to something outside time that characterizes what Johannes Climacus calls Religiousness A. But even a pagan can be religious in this way; it is only in Religiousness B that Christianity properly understood finds its existential expression through a living acceptance of our 'eternal happiness' (as *Crumbs* had put it) being 'based on something historical'. A Christian's actual existence is changed by accepting the 'offence' of this 'contradiction'. In its proper guise, Christianity is the 'only power able truly to arouse offence'. The aim of Christianity is not to bring us cosily together in congregations; it is 'isolating, singling out . . . polemical'.[11] To be properly Christian, we must first 'die' to the world we share, not literally of course, but in the sense Kierkegaard would have read in the fifteenth-century author of *The Imitation of Christ*, the Dutch canon Thomas à Kempis, who quotes Christ as saying to a follower, 'My son, you must needs be ignorant of many things: so consider yourself as dead and crucified to the world.'[12] As Johannes Climacus says, it is now the individual himself that gets in the way. He must 'put himself aside in order to find God'.[13]

*Postscript*'s 'revocation', along with its own preface, *Crumb*'s motto and the postscript to Kierkegaard's very first preface to *From the Papers of One Still Living*, all appear to hang together. A postscript to that earliest preface suggested that the reader might skip the preface or even the entire book. He, the author, would himself take it all back 'into the womb', letting it 'subside once more in the twilight from which it emerged'. Johannes Climacus, in calling his work back, is surely saying, as that astute commentator put it, that he has taken the reader 'to the brink of the bottomless pit of freedom' and 'surprise[d] him with the absolute responsibility he bears for his own life'.[14] Missing from the suggestion is that Johannes Climacus is giving his reader the option of dropping the whole idea.

Understanding the text to be revoked does not mean that, on finding the book on your doorstep, you should throw it away. It says that there would be no point in chasing after whoever left it there, whether to discuss it or to ask what the point was in leaving it there. There is nothing here to argue about; nor is there any point in asking what it is all about. But if you fail to see any point in it, then you *should* throw it away.

Of course, even if you did feel like taking the matter up, you wouldn't find the author anyway. In revoking the work, Johannes Climacus pulls the same vanishing trick that Constantin Constantius performed just by saying so. These were not books for seminars.

*Postscript* leaves the impression that Kierkegaard had a premonition that soon he might not be there either. Especially towards the end, there is a sense of a writer using a last chance to commit himself to print. The character of the work tends increasingly to be that of a container into which all of the important ideas he ever had must be crammed. The huge work was to be pushed out into the world as soon as possible and was delivered 'lock, stock and barrel' to the printer some days before Christmas in 1845. Unusually for a pseudonymous work, Kierkegaard took it there himself. Hitherto his friend J. F. Gjødwad or assistant Israel Levin had acted as his go-between. *Concluding Unscientific Postscript to the Philosophical Crumbs* was published two months later on 27 February 1846, eight months after *Stages*.

There seems little doubt that Kierkegaard really did begin to conceive *Postscript* as the completion of a task he now saw himself as having begun in Berlin in 1841. The nemesis of the Kierkegaard family may have beckoned. In May 1846 he would be 33. In the summer not long after *Stages* had appeared, and following a three-day visit to his brother Peter Christian at Pedersborg, the journal entry dated 10 June 1845 records a visit to his father's grave prompted by an unspecified 'special need'.[15] Now living once more in the family home on Nytorv, inherited together with his brother from their father's estate, sometime between the end of 1844 and the spring of 1846, he wrote instructions for the repair that spring of the family burial site, leaving room on one of the stones for 'Søren Aabye, born 5 May 1813, died ———'. Yet even if he were not to die at the age of 33, exhausted as he must by then have been, he could still escape the 'lies and gossip and vulgarity' by retiring to a country pastorate. Apart from actual ordination, he had qualified himself for such a role. It was a thought that he noted in his journal. In the month following publication of *Postscript*, Kierkegaard wrote,

> My activity as an author, God be praised, is now over. That has been granted me – and next to publishing *Either/Or* this is what I thank God for – to conclude it myself, to understand myself when to stop . . . If only I can manage to become a pastor. Out there, quietly active, allowing myself a little writing in my free time. I shall breathe more easily after all, however much my present life has gratified me.[16]

In the margin to the note recording delivery of the manuscript, Kierkegaard had specified the nature of the 'gossip' and 'vulgarity' that made him hesitate to acknowledge responsibility for the pseudonyms. It was 'in consideration of the circumstances (the *Corsair* nonsense)'. The decision to include the declaration was because he 'owe[d] it to the truth to ignore this kind of thing' and to leave 'the outcome to God's will . . . accepting everything from his hand as a good and perfect gift, scorning to act from prudence, putting my hopes in his giving me a firm and wise spirit.'[17]

The 'everything' that was to follow may have been more than he bargained for when handing the 'compilation' in to the printer 'lock, stock and barrel'. Although this allusion to weaponry is not found in the Danish metaphor (*Rubb og Stubb* – 'with all the bits and pieces'), it conveniently allows one to say that Søren Kierkegaard had by no means shot his bolt. In fact, more writing had already begun. But first, there was the *Corsair* 'nonsense'.

# 8

# The Single Individual

It was in October 1840 that a new liberal periodical had appeared; the *Corsair* was owned and edited by a young writer, Meïr Aaron Goldschmidt, who – then just 21 years old – had begun his journalistic career at the age of seventeen.[1] The paper was an organ of the liberal opposition, effective enough to be confiscated by the censor forty times in Goldschmidt's era, though lately its reputation was more that of a journal for all-around satire and the self-conscious display of wit. Although Kierkegaard was opposed to the paper's avowed liberal policy – and in spite of their differences, besides being close in age – there was something akin to mutual admiration between Goldschmidt and Kierkegaard. Doubtless Goldschmidt saw in Kierkegaard's growing literary reputation a potential ally of the journal's radical cause. He had been one of the few acknowledged figures to praise *Either/Or*. Two years on, he had gone so far as to declare that the name of Victor Eremita would survive when all other Danish writers were forgotten. Kierkegaard not uncharacteristically let this praise go. His objection to the establishment being that it failed to live up to its professed principles, he would have qualms about any suggestion that he was challenging people to overturn them. But what needled him in the undisturbed waters in the wake of *Stages* was that no one, not even the *Corsair*, had shown any interest in this, for him, important revision of the earlier pseudonyms.

An end-of-year entry that never left the journal's pages was in the form of a prayer to the *Corsair* signed 'Victor Eremita'. It included the words, 'Oh, what cruel mercy and forbearance to be branded for all eternity as an inhuman monster because the *Corsair* inhumanly spared one!' It ended, 'Oh! be moved by pity, stay your exalted, cruel grace, and kill me like the rest.'[2]

Shortly after, in late December 1845, with *Postscript* at the printer and proofreading some way ahead, Kierkegaard chanced on a biting criticism of Frater Taciturnus's '"Guilty?" – "Not-Guilty?"', the real crux of *Stages* for him personally. The criticism came in the yearbook *Gæa*, and the review was by one Peder Ludwig Møller, a poet and literary critic with academic ambitions. The review, penetrating as well as caustic, included a capsule version of 'In Vino Veritas'. The sharp tone may have been Møller's way of getting back at Kierkegaard's cursory dismissal of an inquiry addressed to him as Victor Eremita; Møller had only asked if there was anything on his desk that might suit the yearbook.[3] However, since Møller was known as a young man about town and rumoured to be the model for Johannes the Seducer, Kierkegaard's curt refusal might at least have the excuse of indignant propriety. Møller's review concluded that the author of *Stages* must be old and tired, or else highly intelligent but with a morbid imagination. This was nearer the mark than Kierkegaard would have cared to admit, but even closer was Møller's suggestion that it was as if the author wrote from compulsion or as a therapy. Later, Kierkegaard would himself admit to the therapy alternative, while in their sheer volume, the first and the more recent pseudonymous works could easily give the impression of someone writing without being able to stop.

The review stung Kierkegaard into action. As Frater Taciturnus, he wrote an article in *Fædrelandet* with the title 'An Itinerant Aesthetician's Activity, and How He Nevertheless Came to Pay for the Banquet'. To its sigh, 'If only I could soon come in the *Corsair*,' was added the gauntlet-throwing: 'And yet I have already been there; for *ubi spiritus ibi ecclesia: ubi P. L. Møller, ibi* [Where there is spirit there is the church; where there is P. L. Møller, there is] the *Corsair*.'

Meïr Aron Goldschmidt (1819–1887), journalist, novelist and publisher who founded and edited the *Corsair*. After selling the satirical weekly in 1846 due to falling sales, he devoted himself to more serious writing.

Kierkegaard was aware that revealing Møller's connection with the *Corsair* would spoil the young writer's chances with the university, so the savagery was bilateral. That Kierkegaard would then claim to have written his article against Møller 'in much fear and trembling' and had done so, as a conscience-saving insurance policy, on Sundays 'when he also attended church' and 'read a sermon', takes some digesting. But any genuine contrition here could be due to the realization that, with a ruse reminiscent of Machiavelli if not Mephistopheles, he had ruined a young man's chances of a career

Peder Ludvig Møller (1814–1865), a talented literary critic of the Heiberg circle who exerted an influence on Goldschmidt. In 1845, his reputation damaged by Kierkegaard's disclosure of his connection with the *Corsair*, Møller left for Paris. He died in poverty in Rouen twenty years later.

in order just to drum up interest in his own latest pseudonyms. In the event, all he says is that Møller 'took the hint about retiring from the *Corsair* . . . and went off to where he belongs'.[4]

Exit Møller, who was to die in obscurity abroad.[5] Enter the ill-fated clown. A short response by Møller to Taciturnus in *Fædrelandet* was followed on 2 January by an illustrated article in the *Corsair*: 'How the Itinerant Philosopher Found the Itinerant Actual Editor of the *Corsair*'. To this day, the illustrations used by cover designers and conference organizers bear the imprint of the caricatures presented in this and succeeding numbers of the periodical. The caricatures were tame by today's standards but enough to tip the balance of public perception at the time and make Kierkegaard, with his thin legs, apparently awkward gait and uneven trouser-legs, a standing joke. Shunning the immortality offered by the new photographers' studios, for him the result was that, along with

A romantically accented sketch, from about 1840, of Søren Kierkegaard by his half-cousin Niels Christian Kierkegaard (1806–1882), draftsman and lithographer.

other portraits from the time in a romanticizing direction, such distortions became his public image. In Copenhagen the caricatures could be seen for what they were, but even portraits from the time and even more so those 'drawn from memory' bear witness to their lasting effect. For Kierkegaard, it meant the beginning of a period of harassment that would last long enough to make his a household name. Kierkegaard's first biographer, Georg Brandes, could recall that 'when as a child, I failed to pull my trousers down carefully and evenly over . . . my boots, the nanny would admonish me saying, "Søren Kierkegaard!".' His 'vilification', as Kierkegaard called it, reached to all levels of Copenhagen society, and the adult Brandes could remark that the 'caricature drawings of the *Corsair* had made Kierkegaard's legs known in circles where his genius had not penetrated'.[6] In Kierkegaard's own words, he had become fair game for the mockery of any 'butcher's boy' and the 'giggling' and 'simpering' of university students – and yet, as he also observed, his admirers remained overwhelmingly silent.[7]

In a review of his own that he had begun while waiting for the *Postscript* proofs, and still unfinished at the time, Kierkegaard likened these bystanders to a crowd watching a dog that he called 'literary contempt'. It snapped at the heels of anyone who might come along with pretensions to be superior. The process of contempt was one that he called 'levelling' or, as he might have said in reversing the canine metaphor, a matter of bringing the superior person to heel. Once the commotion is over, the watchers remain 'unrepentant' since 'it is not really they who have the dog, they only subscribe'.[8] The review was published under Kierkegaard's own name just a

Caricatures from the *Corsair*: Kierkegaard with the uneven length of his trousers shown; the world revolving around him; Kierkegaard meets the journal's editor.

month after *Postscript* appeared. By the time it was finished, his impatience with a disinterested public had borne fruit: the dog of literary contempt had already begun snapping at his heels.

The book reviewed was a novel, *Two Ages*, published anonymously by Heiberg as 'by the Author of *A Story of Everyday Life*'. The author was Heiberg's mother, Thomasine Gyllembourg or Baroness Thomasine Christine Gyllembourg-Ehrensvärd, the title and surname due to her second husband, a wealthy Swede, who like Heiberg's father was a political exile. On the death of her second husband, Thomasine had moved in with her son, then already establishing his name as a writer, and he had helped to establish hers. His mother became well known anonymously as the author of romances which first appeared in 1827 in her son's newspaper the *Flying Post*. One of these, *An Everyday Story*, became such a success that, like Walter Scott's 'The Author of Waverley', for the remainder of her career, she adopted the name 'The Author of an Everyday Story'. When the son's wife Johanne Luise Pätges, the leading lady of the Danish stage, joined them, they opened the salon whose welcome the 22-year-old Søren Kierkegaard had sought in establishing his own name as a writer.

In 1844 the author of *An Everyday Story* wrote *Two Ages* (*To Tidasldre*), a romance that records a two-generation history in which the first-generation heroine falls in love with a member of the French delegation in Copenhagen, who then leaves to join the army. Time passes, and she believes him to be married if not dead, but they happily reunite when she discovers that he has inherited a large estate in Jutland. The ages in question are the Age of Revolution and the advent of modernity. They are sharply contrasted in the way that Kierkegaard clearly relished: on the one hand, an age of honour, loyalty and passion, and on the other, of prudence, calculation, self-sufficiency and long-term optimism. The latter, the Age of Reason, is seen through the eyes of the fifty-year-old son of the earlier couple, who returns from a long period in America and Europe to find a Copenhagen without legations or any other intimation of 'world-historical catastrophes'. Instead, he discovers, in Kierkegaard's words, a world

> undisturbed by the energetic passion whose form is in its very energy – yes, even in its vehemence – and isn't hiding the power of a secret and forbidden passion. On the contrary, everything is manifestly nondescript, and thus trivial, formless, knowing, coquettish, and openly so. Here there is no great revelation and no deep secret, but superficiality all the more.[9]

It is a world of 'crippling and disheartened, tactless, levelling reciprocity' that is self-generating and empties the place where ideas are properly formed, which is to say in the wills of 'singled-out' selves. The Age of Revolution had indeed passion, but, instead of a singling out, in the heat of revolution, it was on a collective level sustained by slogans; the revolution was a result of action in concert, not of the actions of concerted individuals. In the novel, the scale of the difference in personal involvement could be expressed in the attitudes to marriage. In the Age of Revolution, the 'natural side' of marriage is emancipated from the 'ethically binding one' in a romanticism that has the Frenchman calling his mistress his 'little wife' in spite of their not being married. In the cooler Age of Reason, although the girl still hankers after marriage in a 'pastoral-idyllic' light, her lover thinks the prospect of financial difficulty a good enough reason for breaking off an engagement.

In spite of whatever bearing this had on Kierkegaard's own broken engagement, it is the theme of levelling and the force of envy that occupy him in the final part of the *Review* entitled 'The Results of Observing the Two Ages'. This could be because the dog of literary contempt had already begun snapping at his heels. Himself a victim of levelling, Kierkegaard now diagnoses it as an unstoppable process of spiritual stultification. It may look like a deliberate and humane attempt to achieve 'equality', but, as Kierkegaard says, it is a 'quiet, mathematically abstract affair that avoids all fuss' and proceeds without interference in the one way or the other.[10] Its medium is the public, which is itself a 'monstrous abstraction, indeed [a] phantom' generated by the press.[11]

In 1835 Kierkegaard had accused the liberal press of being a 'nobody'. If you wanted to pin anything on its door there would be no single address to choose from. When it comes to the levelling that Kierkegaard now lays at the door of the public, there is no door at which to lay it.[12]

Cleverer than most but for many doubtless too clever by half, for Kierkegaard himself it was the world that had become too clever.[13] In adulthood, he was now again what he had been in school: an object of fear and, according to his own diagnosis, envy, but an envy that was dispersed in a faceless public. If able to speak, that envy would no doubt have come up with some form of 'sour grapes', as in 'Who wants to be like that!' Later, when Kierkegaard became terminally ill, the hitherto-vaporized envy would condense into venomous drops in the pens or mouths of those who could then feel safer in asserting their own superiority, though even then usually only among themselves. One such communication talks of 'an acute ice-cold spirit whose words are as sharp as icicles' and of Kierkegaard as a 'false prophet' with a 'passionate desire to be noticed' that was doubtless the 'root cause' of his 'illness'.[14] This was when Kierkegaard was indeed ill after a frontal attack on the Church, still seven years away.

By then, in his prolonged privacy, Kierkegaard had become a pervasive presence in the way only absent people can be, unavailable but also immune to the 'chatter' that the *Review* said was a feature of an 'essentially sensible, reflective, dispassionate' age that lacked any steady aim and was consequently 'eruptive in its fleeting enthusiasms'.[15] Other features of the de-spiritualizing age are formlessness, superficiality, flirtation and the need to 'reason things out', all of them failures to make and then face the 'passionate' distinctions out of which character and morality are formed.[16] Meanwhile, there would be an intense period of outer calm and inner tumult.

Four weeks following the publication of *A Literary Review*, Kierkegaard paid another brief visit to Berlin. It would be his last. Perhaps he just wanted to escape Copenhagen's now-less-friendly streets. The latter can be illustrated by encounters with Goldschmidt both before and after the caricatures. The two had first met at the Rørdams' in 1837 and had been on friendly terms. Kierkegaard had encouraged Goldschmidt to take up comic composition in a Heibergian spirit as a worthy art form. They were even walking arm in arm in the street when Kierkegaard first brought up the subject of P. L. Møller and the article in *Gæa*. On their last encounter, however, as Goldschmidt recalled, Kierkegaard had 'walked by' him with 'an extremely embittered look'. Goldschmidt's eye for the comical was sharp enough to see some sign of it even in the 'bitterness of that look'. But then there was something comical in Kierkegaard's 'entire personal presence' in any case. It was easy to make fun of him. And yet Goldschmidt could see something else. The comic aspect 'slipped aside' and gave way to 'something elevated and ideal' that he could also see in Kierkegaard's personality.

> There was something in that intense, wild look that in a way drew the curtain aside from the higher court on which Kierkegaard had until then prided himself, and which I had been unable, but also unwilling to see in spite of certainly seeing its presence.[17]

By October Goldschmidt had become sufficiently anguished over his role in the *Corsair* affair to resign. But, for Kierkegaard, the damage was done. In his journal, he wrote of how much he missed being able to 'roam about in the streets and be nothing, while thoughts and ideas worked within me'.[18] A year after the original exchange, he could still tell of sniggering youths in church.

Yet had it not been Kierkegaard himself who had unleashed the snapping dog? Perhaps, but showing that it was there to be unleashed was a valuable indicator of how low the spiritual barometer in Denmark had sunk. There might be a constructive design in it all, even a divine plan. The suffering that Kierkegaard had brought upon himself could then be a rite of passage required for getting through to the truth of Christianity, even a necessary condition of actually *being* a Christian.

That thought kept Kierkegaard's pen busy for the remaining years of his life. The direction had changed. During the last almost five years he had been posing questions, more questions than people normally liked to ask. His attitude had been that of the Johannes Climacus who in *Postscript* said that, for him, having been a student for a 'half-score of years' and 'accomplished nothing', in a world where everyone was trying to make things easier, it was time 'to make difficulties everywhere'.[19] But now, no longer the destructive ironist playing a Socratic hand in loosening minds of their de-spiritualizing habits, Kierkegaard was close to finding a cause that he felt had to be preached. In that *Postscript* summary of the pseudonymous works, including his own, Johannes Climacus claims that these 'to the very last have honestly abstained from lecturing'.[20] The time had now come for something quite close to that.

Kierkegaard left for Berlin on the day before his 33rd birthday. On arrival, he chanced on a distant relative and long-time admirer, Hans Brøchner, seven years younger but on close enough terms with Kierkegaard for the latter to invite him to dine at his hotel. There, Brøchner could observe how 'ingeniously' Kierkegaard had arranged his rooms 'in order to encourage the mood'.[21] We don't know what mood Kierkegaard had in mind, nor for what reflections the mood was designed. But regarding the latter, two possibilities are worth airing. One is that he was encouraging a mood of high-minded concern for others that could lead to *Works of Love*. Was it just a coincidence that the reason for his later relief at money problems forcing him to cancel yet another trip to Berlin was that travel at that point would have broken his mood and *Works of Love* would not have been completed? The other possibility is that the environment he needed was one in which he could struggle with a question of principle: namely, his status as a religious writer – not, be it noted, a writer *on* religion but a writer who *is* religious and writes as such.

In 1872, long after Kierkegaard's death, a collection of papers was published under the title *The Book on Adler*. Adler, the same Adolph Peter whose dissertation on Hegel had attracted Kierkegaard's attention before he settled down to writing his own, had at one time been a priest on the island of Bornholm. In 1843, after publishing several controversial tracts in which he claimed to have received divine revelation directly from Christ, Adler was pensioned off and generally considered a crank. On receiving a visit, Kierkegaard found Adler to be highly intelligent, if 'ecstatic', but it would be unfortunate if readers of what Kierkegaard now planned to write saw him in the same light. Perhaps due to their topic, his thoughts on Adler were not as clear and sharp as they would be were his wit given free play. Nor was the problem here one with which any new 'blessed children' could help him. The last part of Kierkegaard's *Book on Adler* is a refutation of the very idea of direct revelation, but the motive for writing it was Kierkegaard's need to ask what *other* kind of authority there could be and how *he* could claim it. The question was to crop up continually over the following years, during which, in a series of rented apartments following the sale of the family home, Kierkegaard stood more than ever stooped over his desk – a desk that not only looked not unlike a lectern but functioned rather like one, too, and at times might even be mistaken for a pulpit.

A real pulpit was no longer on the cards. Sometime before November 1846, Kierkegaard, still thinking of a move into the country, had talked to Bishop Mynster. He knew that the latter's attitude to religion was not so unlike his own; they agreed that philosophy and Christianity should be kept apart, and both had a distaste for the Grundtvigians. For Mynster, the church as an oasis for 'quiet hours' beyond the reach of the 'noise of the world' and 'worldly affairs' was no place for extrovert congregationalism.[22] Kierkegaard, though not yet opposing the Church as such, was hoping quite unrealistically to infect Mynster enough with his sense of what Christianity really meant to bring him over to his side. Mynster's 'quiet hours' gave respite from worldly affairs but, for Kierkegaard, these affairs could do with some Christian engagement. At the very least, there was a need for a clergy who treated their callings as more than a worldly affair. Mynster, for his own part, appeared not to oppose Kierkegaard's plan to go out into the country to preach there. However, Kierkegaard soon suspected that this was because Mynster wanted him out of the way. He had read that Mynster even suggested Kierkegaard had some political kinship with the subversive Goldschmidt. In 1847 Kierkegaard wrote that Mynster, 'in spite of harbour[ing] certain feelings of benevolence for me, perhaps in his quiet moments even more than he admits', saw him as a 'suspicious and even dangerous person'.[23]

Withdrawal to the country at that point would, of course, also make people think he was fleeing the fray. Kierkegaard chose now to look at it in another way: the fray would put him on the warpath – albeit only metaphorically insofar as the war would be waged in the writer's treadmill.

God be praised that all the rabble's barbaric attacks have landed on me. I have now really had time to learn inwardly and convince myself that it was after all a melancholy idea to want to live out in a country parsonage and do penance in seclusion and oblivion. Now I am ready to go and determined as never before.[24]

The primate of Denmark, Jacob P. Mynster (1775–1854), photographed in 1850.

March 1847 saw *Edifying Discourses in a Different Tenor* and September *Works of Love*. In April 1848 came *Christian Discourses*, and by November Kierkegaard would have finished his posthumously published 'report to history', *The Point of View for My Work as an Author*. In 1849 came *The Lily of the Field and the Bird of the Air*, along with *Two Minor Ethical-religious Treatises*, published within five days of each other in May, and in June another pseudonymous work, *The Sickness Unto Death*, was completed, to be followed in November by *Three Discourses at Communion on Friday*s. A compilation under the new pseudonym Anti-Climacus appeared in 1850: *Practice in Christianity*, followed in December by *An Edifying Discourse*.

Kierkegaard's signed works have, on the whole, received less attention than those under pseudonyms. But some commentators consider *Works of Love*, written as a series of 'deliberations' rather than discourses, to be Kierkegaard's most significant philosophical

achievement. Both it and *The Lily of the Field and the Bird of the Air*
stand out not only stylistically, but in the way they develop different
aspects of the 'single individual'. No longer his own single 'dear
reader', it now became a 'category', the one that Kierkegaard was
soon to claim as his most lasting achievement as a writer. From a
religious perspective, he was now looking in his authorship for a
generally applicable unifying principle, the lack of which he had
always criticized in others and more than ten years earlier had
anxiously sought in his own person.

In revising some of the older journals, he found in one from 1839,
which otherwise contained nothing 'felicitous or accomplished', a
brief entry on marriage not being true love. He notes that he could
well have used this in the recently completed *Works of Love*.[25] The
time of that earlier entry had been one of personal agonizing and
lost religious motivation. With the future complicated also by the
image of his 'heart's sovereign mistress', he had said at the time that
marriage was a unity in 'sensate form' and not 'in spirit and truth'.
At this point, it was the impossibility of becoming one *spirit* that
troubled him, and its relevance for *Works of Love* is clear enough
when true or Christian love is taken to be some form of a loving
relationship between 'single individuals'. From his writing desk,
Kierkegaard now saw 'the evolution of the whole world' tending
'in the direction of the absolute significance of the category of the
particular . . . precisely the principle of Christianity'. But to become
singular, to be really 'singled out' in the terms of the *Review*, requires
'ethical [and] religious courage'.[26]

Of *Works of Love*, Kierkegaard says that it was written not to
'assuage and comfort' but to 'arouse and vex'. Its power to do the
latter is due not only to the way in which it turns our concepts
upside down by putting the single individual in the centre. Ten years
earlier, he had commented on what petit bourgeois parents believed
it means to say 'love thy neighbour' with regard to their children's
upbringing ('these well brought-up children, now useful members

of the state . . . highly susceptible to every passing influenza of emotion' but trained in such decorous expressions as 'have the goodness to . . .' and 'with great pleasure').[27] In the second of the two series of deliberations, it becomes clear from *Works of Love* that love in the Christian sense would not only outrage bourgeois sensibilities but, by quite normal standards, make the Christian look a fool. The Christian must assume the possibility of love in any other person's heart. The first series makes it clear, however, that the real topic here is not 'love' but 'works' of love. A work of love is not open and above board; nor does it aspire to be mutual in the way worldly wisdom would expect. Works of love belong in a context of polemics and awakening; for love to be 'working' is for love to build love in another. It is a *work* of love in the Christian sense only if it is prepared to build love in *any* other, just as one finds him or her. To love one person rather than another is a matter of preference and implies sensate gratification on the lover's part. Should anything that makes the other attractive change in a way that makes the love vanish, the love was not Christian. Even in sacrificing oneself for the beloved, no doubt something that most consider an ultimate act in the other's interest, the thought that the sacrifice is *mine* implies an element of self-love.

Clearly, in most of its admitted aspects, Kierkegaard's love of Regine would fail the Christian test as he saw it. But there is little doubt that he was 'working' with his love for her in this conceptually revolutionary direction. It is not beyond belief that these more than 350 pages of deliberation were part of that process, in addition, that is, to bringing clearer light to the faith of his father.

Just as *Works of Love* appeared, Kierkegaard's publisher informed him that *Either/Or* had sold out and a new edition was needed. This put Kierkegaard into a spin; a two-volume work read mainly for its first volume and most of all 'The Seducer's Diary' had placed him well outside the religious sphere in the public consciousness. To discourage the focus on the 'Diary', he now insisted on a single-volume edition to be accompanied with *The Point of View for My Work as an Author*. The latter would be postponed and, as the required makeweight, Kierkegaard published the unambiguously religious *The Lily of the Field and the Bird of the Air*.

Pointing not at the other as the object of Christian love, this work is directed at ourselves. Christ commands that we be 'like' those lilies and birds (Matthew 6:25–34), for they 'neither toil nor spin' nor do they 'sow'. Without the worries that give rise to our unending questions of moral principle and choice, they are examples or perhaps inspiring images of what it is to be following God's will with unalloyed joy. For after all, 'what is it to be joyful?'

> It is truly to be present to oneself; but truly to be present to oneself is this 'today', this to *be* today, truly to *be today*. And the truer it is that you *are* today, the more you are entirely present to yourself in being today, the less does tomorrow, the day of misfortune, exist for you. Joy is the present time, with the entire emphasis falling on *the present time*. That is why God is blessed, he who eternally says: 'Today', he who is eternally and infinitely present to himself in being today. And that is why the lily and the bird are joy, because by silence and unconditional obedience they are entirely present to themselves in being today.[28]

The 'three Godly discourses' forming this work are a challenge to look at your life as if it were for you,

> that you came into existence, that you exist, that 'today' you receive the necessities of existence, that you came into existence, that you became a human being, that you can see . . . hear . . . have a sense of smell . . . a sense of taste, that you can feel; that the sun shines for you and for your sake . . .[29]

It sounds as if Mynster's 'quiet hour' is being brought out into the everyday from which the bishop believed the church was a necessary escape.

The 'category of the single individual' is introduced in the unpublished *Point of View*, with Kierkegaard seeming to believe that it had been granted him by circumstances that were divinely appointed. By sweeping away the scenarios in which lives blur the nakedness and isolation of a self-conscious being such as we are, his suffering had given him privileged access to what that really means. Any importance attached to him as a writer depended on his being right on this score but also on his acting accordingly. He writes in his journal, 'If only this was the right category, if what was said about it was in order, if I perceived it correctly and understood properly that this was my task . . . then I stand and my writings with me.'[30] In its concluding 'Two Notes', *The Point of View* presents the single individual as the thread connecting the earlier pseudonyms with these religious writings. Beginning in *Either/Or* with the idea of 'exceptionality' as an inability to 'realize the universal', it ends in 'the single individual' as the 'category through which in a religious sense [his own] time, history itself and the human race must pass.'[31] Where the focus in the first four-and-a-half years had been literary, with the membrane of pseudonym keeping him officially out of the fray however much of his own life had gone into it, Kierkegaard now saw himself as having written himself *into* his works. In his enforced seclusion, he would make it clear, however, that his theme is *not* himself or anything that *he* can represent, or for which he might seek 'disciples': 'The single individual can mean the most unique of all or it can mean each and every one.'[32] The early pseudonymous works are said to be 'deceptions' because they adopted a position lower than that 'back' to which they were said to be designed to lead the reader. The 'maieutic purpose' of his writing had not been to 'lead' the reader *to* the author himself in any 'empirical' sense but to the 'single individual' in an 'ideal sense'.[33]

It is in *The Point of View* that Kierkegaard admits to having from childhood been 'in the grip of an enormous depression'. He speaks of the compulsion to write which elsewhere he takes to have been a form of cure: 'Only when I am productive do I feel well.'[34] That admission can be linked to the reason Kierkegaard gives for not publishing this 'report' in his lifetime; he said there was something 'untrue about it'. Part of the untruth was this notion of deception; it had been less deliberate than the word suggests. Kierkegaard had been educating himself on the way. Just as important, however, was the distance between his person and what these later works represented.

Kierkegaard's pseudonymity is sometimes taken to be a form of open deceit, in that the real author consciously 'adopts' various points of view that are not his own. It is significant that it was often and even typically the case that, from 1843 on, Kierkegaard chose pseudonymity at the last moment. One may easily imagine the enthusiasm with which his writing transported him to positions that he felt he genuinely embodied at the time of writing, for him then to realize, when the work was done, that they were not exactly how he could claim to see things in the light of day. He might also see how troublesome it might be, as well as deceitful, to be identified with the result. That this was the case with *The Sickness Unto Death* is openly admitted. That work was at first planned as the first part of a volume containing deliberately 'vexing' material to include an essay entitled 'An Attempt to Introduce Christianity into Christendom'. That he plucked a new pseudonym, 'Anti-Climacus', out of the air, a 'Christian to an extraordinary degree', and only at the last minute, suggests that although the intention to vex was heartfelt, the result was not one that he could claim to stand for in person.[35] The book presents a typology of despair that collects, and distinguishes between, the innumerable public identities that individuals adopt to escape the inherent nakedness of the self-conscious souls that we are, the true 'ground zero' from which faith and any hope of salvation must begin. In all its configurations, 'despair' here means failing and, in the end, deliberately refusing to see this. But the 'ground zero' metaphor is incomplete. What one despairs of is not simply being more than nothing, a hole in the ground as it were; the despair is over the possibility of the forgiveness of sins.[36] Thus *The Sickness Unto Death* can be seen to mark the end of that promised journey from its author's consciousness to the 'preconditions' of a sin whose origin *The Concept of Anxiety* told its readers is repeated in every dawning consciousness of self. Salvation means faith and faith means works – not words, but works. Ideally, it means acting in imitation of Christ as presented in *Practice in Christianity*.

In these 'working' terms, the journey was not one that Kierkegaard had completed. He had pushed himself 'only to the point of being a perfectly simple Christian', although, merely because he realized that this was the case, he would be 'one of the few' upon whom a strong remedy like *Practice in Christianity* might work. Yes, he had been able to 'situate' Christianity in the domain of 'reflection', but the task was not one that he could take to be divinely appointed.[37] The thought that it might be so had been his own: it could in no way be considered a revelation placed in him by God. He 'reproached' himself for any 'attempts at self-aggrandizement' that had crept into 'previous entries in this journal' but felt that God would forgive him.[38]

# 9

# Thief and Martyr

Coming to terms with the moral implications of the break with
Regine had taken almost five years of intensive as well as extensive
writing. That Regine still lingered in his mind ten years later is
beyond doubt. Seven years after their engagement, he had gone
out of town on the day she married Fritz Schlegel. The rift was still
one he wanted to repair, in his own mind ostensibly for reasons
that were religious. Although fearing that his intervention at this
point might disturb a quite conventional marriage by reawakening
Regine's desires in his direction, Kierkegaard at the same time saw
in Regine's marriage an opportunity to approach her on a higher
plane. In his journals he describes his own early captivation as an
interference in his relationship to God. There was now a chance
to include Regine in that relationship.[1]

Any fears Kierkegaard entertained about the married couple's
response to his all-too transparent attempts to appear a scoundrel
were in any case groundless. Had he only known Fritz and Regine
had been reading his works aloud to each other even during their
engagement. They continued reading him (Kierkegaard sent her all
his discourses) after they married, and on Kierkegaard's death,
Schlegel would immediately buy a copy of the *Posthumous Papers*.[2]
Later still, on seeing portraits of Grundtvig and Kierkegaard side
by side while being shown round a hospital of whose board he was
chairman, Fritz turned to the entourage and said of Kierkegaard, 'Long
after Grundtvig's influence is over and done, his will still be alive!'[3]

The comment (recalling Goldschmidt's about Victor Eremita) must have delighted Regine. It showed that the difficulties Fritz had endured from Kierkegaard were not her husband's fault. Thinking quite insanely that he could leave matters of unity in 'sensate form' to Schlegel, while he and Regine continued their relationship in 'spirit and truth', Kierkegaard had at one time planned to approach Schlegel with this impractical scheme in mind. The opportunity arose on the death in June 1849 of Regine's father, a man Kierkegaard much respected. The previous summer, Kierkegaard had tried to contact him in order to make amends. It was in the late summer of 1848 that he drove on an impulse to Fredensborg, where the Olsens had a summer residence, with a premonition of meeting the family there. Sure enough, he ran into Counsellor Olsen, but with 'tears in his eyes', and in a voice of 'stifled passion', Regine's father said he did not wish to speak to him. When Kierkegaard protested, the older man turned and ran off with such agility that, 'even if I'd wanted,' recorded Kierkegaard, 'it would have been impossible for me to catch up'.[4] A year after the still-athletic counsellor had fled from him, and once the printer had been given the go-ahead for *The Sickness Unto Death*, Kierkegaard wrote to Schlegel asking for an opportunity to converse with his wife. Fritz, understandably opposed to any interference in his marriage, declined and returned unopened a letter Kierkegaard had enclosed for Regine concerning their relationship, saying it might help her.[5]

Despite those previous two productive years, Kierkegaard had been forced at the time to take care of several 'worldly affairs'. The family home had been sold in December 1847, but with a clause allowing Kierkegaard a room there until Easter 1848, when he could move to another apartment. There had been two visits to his brother, now remarried and pastor at Pedersborg near Sorø, some distance from Copenhagen. As *Works of Love* neared completion, sheer fatigue overtook him, prompting those thoughts of yet another spell abroad, but which his financial worries forced him to cancel.

The year 1848 was a year of turmoil in Europe, with the February Revolution in Paris and the Vienna Uprising in October. Denmark also became involved. Prussia engaged in a conflict over Denmark's control over the duchies of Schleswig and Holstein. One-third of the Danish population at that time was German-speaking. The Napoleonic Wars had raised the level of national feeling and one result of the conflict was that Denmark finally became a constitutional monarchy. Since the actual hostilities took place in southern Jutland, Copenhagen was left unscathed except for those who had to pay taxes levied for the war. Kierkegaard financed the publication of his own works and gave quite a number away. Only *Either/Or* really sold. He was then forced to wrestle with the printer over the cost of the new edition. When he moved into a newly built apartment in Rosenborggade, he took in a lodger. His manservant Anders having been drafted into service made life, and in particular moving, more difficult. Yet regarding his own project, he later reported that it had been a crucial year; it was one in which he saw that he could step into that project in person, or 'act in character', as he put it. It was the year the three 'Godly discourses' and *The Sickness Unto Death* appeared.

Seeing what project Kierkegaard might enter into 'in character' is not easy. He was, he said, a simple Christian and made no claim even to have attempted to satisfy the requirement that, in his brief (editor's) preface to *Practice*, he says the pseudonymous author has 'forced up' to a 'supreme ideality'.[6] There was, however, his suffering. That was genuine enough and something into which he could claim to have entered into his project in character. Not quite imitating Christ in this respect, his own suffering was something he nevertheless tended to liken to that of the persecuted Christians and he tended to define Christianity in the light of that experience rather than just marking its birth pangs. Of course, just writing about suffering would not be enough. Indeed, writing had been a kind of balm – a blessing even – and at any rate an escape from his melancholia.

Still, writing with the intensity he had recently shown had taken its bodily toll. An increasing emphasis on physical suffering is found in the journals at this time. On completing *The Point of View*, he had been 'quite exhausted'. The 'spirit' was 'strong enough but regrettably all too strong for my body'. It helped him to endure 'such a sickly state of health', but in another way its strength 'overwhelmed [the] body'.[7] In 1848 Kierkegaard noted that his 'physical powers' were in decline and the state of his health 'varied terribly', so much so that he doubted whether he would 'live to see the publication of the really decisive works' including *The Sickness Unto Death*.[8]

Bodily suffering for the truth can easily speak martyrdom. Kierkegaard, in his continuing struggles, came up with a summary version of what he had concluded so far. In a piece called 'On the Difference between a Genius and an Apostle', he says that apostles are not born but called by God to 'proclaim the doctrine and use the authority'. He is quite sure he is not an apostle: 'Good God, instead of helping to honour Christianity I would have ruined it.' As a genius, he might exemplify Christianity, but then again, 'as an author I am a rather odd kind of genius – neither more nor less, with no authority at all'. He was therefore constantly under instructions to 'annihilate himself' in order 'not to become an authority for anyone'. Although 'I am,' as he says, 'a genius who might be martyred for the truth, I am not capable of being a martyr for Christianity, for I cannot call myself a Christian to that degree.'[9] By the time he published this essay, along with a companion piece, 'Has a Human Being the Right to Let Himself Be Put to Death for the Truth?', Kierkegaard's writing can remind us of that early call for an idea for whose truth he would be willing to live and die.

Beyond the desk, however, there was still some living to be done. In the spring of 1851, Kierkegaard moved for the first time outside the city walls and made his home in a second-floor apartment in a villa in what was then a semi-rural area on the outskirts of Copenhagen. From there, he took regular walks into town.

On these excursions, he encountered Regine, or rather they passed by each other, but never spoke. The encounters were frequent, as Kierkegaard records in his journal. In May 1852, he writes,

> During the latter part of 1851 she encountered me every day. It was during the period when I would walk home by way of Langelinie at ten o'clock in the morning. The timing was exact and the place merely shifted farther and farther up the road to the limekiln. She came walking as if from the limekiln . . . That was how it went, day after day.[10]

Garff frames these wordless encounters in a language of mutual erotic excitement rather than as the rehearsal of an old habit. He points to Kierkegaard's painstaking descriptions of the meetings, noting distance, changes of route and even wind direction.[11] But in whatever way they are seen, there is in these ritual encounters just a touch of *The Lily of the Field and the Bird of the Air*. By avoiding words, the two can live in an eternal present plucked out of time, forgetting for a brief moment the 'everyday' obstructions to their union, including Regine's marriage.

Already in January 1850, Kierkegaard could write that for over a month they had 'seen each other almost every blessed day, or at least twice every other day'.[12] How long this had been going on is not clear, nor is the precise mood of the meeting – or maybe it was not precise, something between a bad conscience and unfulfilled dream, deep-freezing the past to keep a duty for redress alive in the one case, and in the other, a desire to console a youngish man now grown prematurely old and who had been mocked by her fellow citizens. In wordless encounters, there is no insistent either/or; on the contrary, for these two, who have kept each other in mind for so long without becoming properly acquainted, if the actual world could be put in abeyance for a second or two, the meetings could presage exciting possibilities. They may have begun by accident, but repetitions began to be hoped for and eventually planned, in the end too successfully for comfort. By 1852 Kierkegaard had moved back inside the walls to a two-room apartment, which was let out of a larger apartment opposite the Church of Our Lady at 5–6 Klædeboderne, now 28 Skindergade and 5 Dyrkøb. It was to be his last address. But the meetings with Regine continued and seemed on the point of becoming too much. On 1 January 1852 Kierkegaard decided that he must change his route:

> I went home by way of Nørreport. Some time passed in this fashion, and we did not see each other. One morning she encountered me on the path by the lake, where I was now in the habit of walking. The next day I also took this path, which was my usual one. She was not there. As a precaution, however, I nonetheless changed my future route and went down Farimags-Veien, and finally I varied my homeward route . . . But what happened? Some time had passed. Then she meets me one morning at 8 o'clock on the avenue outside Østerport, the route I walk to Cph every morning.[13]
>
> The next day she was not there, however. I continued walking to town by this same route, which I cannot very well alter. So she met me here quite often, sometimes also on the ramparts, the path I take to town. Perhaps it was coincidence, perhaps. I could not understand what she was doing on that route at that hour there, but as I notice everything, I noticed that she came that way especially if there was an east wind. So indeed, it could be because she could not bear the east wind on Langelinie. But – she did also come when there was a west wind.[14]

They met again on his 39th birthday.

> As a rule, I am always away on my birthday, but I was not feeling quite well. So I stayed at home; as usual I walked into town, to

Kierkegaard drawn from life in the period 1853–5 by H. P. Hansen (1829–1899), known for his portraits and book illustrations.

talk with the doctor because I had considered celebrating my birthday with something new, something I had never tasted before, castor oil. Right outside my door, on the sidewalk in front of the avenue, she meets me. As so often happens of late, I cannot keep from smiling when I see her – ah, how much she has come to mean to me! – she smiled in return and nodded. I took a step past her, then raised my hat and walked on.[15]

It was not until 17 March 1855 that the fourteen years of silence would be broken. Fritz Schlegel had been appointed governor of the Danish West Indies for a five-year period; the date of the encounter was the same as that of their departure. In the morning, Regine, before embarking on that strenuous journey, went out into the streets to look for the old young man in the broad-brimmed hat. She found him. As she passed him, she said under her breath, 'God bless you – may it go well with you!' As Garff comments,

For just an instant, that Saturday meeting in a random Copenhagen street turned everything upside down. Regine's

Photograph of Regine Schlegel, probably taken just before leaving for the West Indies in 1855.

blessing succeeded in rendering speechless a man never otherwise at a loss for the right words. Kierkegaard was here exposed to a situation of the kind one might describe with antiquated words like 'dispensation' and 'visited upon', words with which one fumbles to articulate the sense that the most potent things in life always come from the other, they are not at one's beck and call or in one's own power to effect. What went through the master-thinker theologian's mind in that moment of blessing, no one knows. Perhaps, just for once, there was no thought in his mind at all, simply acceptance of this blessing from the woman in his life.[16]

That she had this status is more than demonstrated by a rosewood cabinet made according to Kierkegaard's instructions in response to Regine's statement – as the engagement disintegrated – that her whole life she would thank him if only she could stay – even if it meant living in a little cupboard. The cabinet was built without shelves to allow space and contained special editions of his works and everything that might remind him of her.[17]

By 1851 Kierkegaard's creative work was in one sense done. It was the year in which those silent meetings were first noted. Indeed, his own 'development' or 'education' had already been completed in 1846 with *Postscript*. Everything later, except for a short piece called 'The Crisis (and a Crisis) in the Life of an Actress', was written at the point of arrival. That exception can be seen in just this light. In one way, he was discharging a social debt to Madame Heiberg, who had performed the role of Juliet to great acclaim nineteen years after her breakthrough in that role. It was also to please his friend Giødwad, the editor who asked him to write the essay. But the main reason was that here Kierkegaard saw a chance to correct his public image. Now that his writing had taken a decidedly religious turn, he was worried that people might think he was going 'saintly' under the pressure of criticism. More important still – indeed, 'vitally important' – was a need to pre-empt the 'heresy' that his own religiousness was 'the sort of thing one turns to in old age'.

Thoughts of an official position were renewed, now with conflict rather than repose in mind. The idea would be to work against the evils of 'Christendom' from within. Kierkegaard was still attending Mynster's sermons, but although he agreed with Mynster's words, he felt the need to add the 'stronger accent' that he firmly believed to reside in his own 'distinctness'. The Grundtvigians claimed already to be Christians of the strict kind, so that where the 'Right Reverend old-timer' aimed too low, the latter failed laughably to reach the high level they claimed for themselves. The scene had begun to be set for a confrontation, and Kierkegaard's journals now became a forge for the honing of his weapons for a conflict to come. Several of the themes that would later appear in an attack on the Church make their first appearance in *Judge for Yourself*, including what it really means to be a witness to the truth. *Practice in Christianity* had already – much to Mynster's annoyance – called for the introduction of Christianity into Christendom.

Mynster died just six months later, on 30 January 1854. The memorial address at the funeral ceremony in the Royal Chapel on 5 March was given by Professor Martensen, who had become court chaplain. Mynster's death installed him in the ranks of those who were witnesses to the truth. Because the memorial came from Martensen in that setting – and on an occasion in which religion took on the form of theatre even more blatantly than usual – no more was needed. Kierkegaard immediately sat down and wrote an article, 'Was Bishop Mynster a "Witness to the Truth," One of the "Proper Witnesses to the Truth" – is *This the Truth*?'. For reasons that are not entirely clear, he withheld its publication until the end of the year. One explanation would be the usual scruple about preventing his own opposition from being confused with others'. Martensen was not the only candidate suggested as a possible successor to Mynster, and it would be misleading if Kierkegaard's opposition to the Church were seen merely to be his objection to a particular candidacy for its top position. Another explanation for delaying publication might be consideration for Regine.[18] He would not want to have her associated in people's minds with what they saw as his religious iconoclasm. That Kierkegaard waited until she had left Copenhagen for the West Indies before delivering his most telling cannonade speaks in its favour.

When Regine left Copenhagen for the West Indies on that silence-breaking Saturday, 17 March 1855, Kierkegaard was already (as Hans Brøchner put it) 'bringing out his big guns'. He had 'opened up his batteries in an article in *Fædrelandet*' to be followed later by 'a sort of journal called *The Moment*'.[19] The article in December had already called Mynster 'weak, addicted to pleasure and great only as a declaimer'. A real witness is a man whose life from first to last is unacquainted with everything called enjoyment . . . A witness for the truth is a man who witnesses for the truth in poverty – in poverty, in lowliness and abasement, so unappreciated, hated, detested, so mocked, insulted, laughed to scorn . . . A witness for the truth, one of the authentic witnesses for the truth, is a man who is scourged, maltreated, dragged from one prison to another . . . and then at last . . . crucified, or beheaded, or burned, or broiled roasted on a grill, his lifeless body thrown away by the assistant executioner in a remote place, unburied – this is how a witness for the truth is buried![20]

The article called on the Church to admit that this was the right description. Not unexpectedly, the Church failed to do that, and Kierkegaard published another article in *Fædrelandet* at the end of January, repeating his challenge but in 'stronger' terms:

I hereby repeat my objection: I would rather gamble, booze, wench, steal, and murder rather than take part in making a fool of God, would rather spend my days in the bowling alley, in the billiard parlor, my nights in games of chance or at masquerades than participate in the kind of earnestness Bishop Martensen calls Christian earnestness.[21]

It was after the Schlegels had left in mid-March that a series of 22 articles began to appear in *Fædrelandet*, one of them on Martensen's accession as primate. It instructed the new bishop to put an end to the charade or 'official untruth' that what they preached was the Christianity of the New Testament. The articles continued until the end of March.

Instead of provoking instant reaction, the articles met only incomprehension. Why had it taken so long? But also what was the point in desecrating the memory of a noble anti-Hegelian and friend of the family? The family had also been shocked. Although Kierkegaard held his cards close to his chest in public, he had no qualms about venting his feelings about Mynster on his brother-in-law Ferdinand Lund. According to Troels Frederik Troels-Lund, Kierkegaard's visits proved to be acutely embarrassing to the Lund family, and they did all they could to get Uncle Søren to talk of other things. The climax came one day when Lund's wife Anna Cathrine got up and said,

> You know that the man you speak so ill of is one for whom
> we here cherish the greatest respect and profoundest gratitude.
> I cannot sit here and hear him continually abused. If you don't
> stop the only way I can avoid it is by leaving the room.

And with that, she departed.[22] On looking back at these visits, Troels-Lund, the youngest son of the remarried Lund (first married to Petrea), saw them as a deliberate exercise for what was to come. When it did come, among the words used by Kierkegaard's former teachers were 'sickly', 'ecstatic', 'sectarian' and 'unjust'. Madame Heiberg, a long-standing admirer and subject of that essay on a crisis in the life of an actress, called him a 'faithless beast'.[23]

The final onslaught began on 24 May 1855 with the appearance of the first of nine numbers of that 'sort of journal' *The Moment*. This was a pamphlet financed by Kierkegaard himself in which he pilloried the Church and a clergy intent only on a comfortable living and whose amenities depended on preaching a cut-price form of Christianity that only made a fool of God. In the first, there was a piece about the bad taste left in people's mouths by his *Fædrelandet* articles. He advised them to take an emetic. In another number, priests, instead of blessing couples in marriage, should really be persuading them not to marry, since all they were doing is blessing a desire that produces children under the pretext that, because these will be born in Christendom, the young parents are performing the good deed of producing more Christians. Baptism and confirmation are just a farce and the Church itself a stage. Another issue treats the New Testament as a travel guide read in the cigar-smoking comfort of a railway dining car, describing the passing landscape as a ravine full of hideouts for robbers ready to beat up travellers. The Church is likened to a hospital in which attempted improvements in treatment cannot prevent patients from dying like flies, because it is the building itself that is at fault. In this scrapheap of a state church – which, spiritually speaking, has been left unventilated in time out of mind – the enclosed air has turned toxic.

> Then let this pile of rubbish tumble down, get rid of it, close all these boutiques and booths . . . and let us once again worship God in simplicity instead of making a fool of him in splendid edifices; let us be in earnest again and stop playing . . .[24]

Kierkegaard said that what he wanted was 'honesty' and claimed he had just one 'thesis': Christianity simply did not exist. It was no wonder that, in a land where Christianity had become 'naturalized' to the extent of being a comforting ritual enacted out of habit, Kierkegaard's personally begotten religious perspective made him an outsider. A remark made five years earlier compared his life as a loner with that of his sister's husband's palaeontologist brother Peter Wilhelm Lund in Brazil:

> Today it occurred to me that my life resembles his. Just as he lives in Brazil, lost to the world, condemned to excavating antediluvian fossils, so I live as though I were outside the world, condemned to excavating Christian concepts.[25]

God was not dead but was being made to look a fool. The ninth number of *The Moment* appeared on 24 September 1855. The tenth was ready for printing when Kierkegaard died. In that number's

# Øieblikket.

## Nr. 9.

Andet Oplag.

### Indhold:

21 Septbr. 1855.     S. Kierkegaard.

Kjøbenhavn.
Forlagt af C. A. Reitzels Bo og Arvinger.
Bianco Lunos Bogtrykkeri.

The contents page of the last published issue of *The Moment*, 21 September 1855. On 2 October Kierkegaard collapsed on the street; on 11 November he died.

penultimate section, Kierkegaard had written that his 'task' was Socratic: 'I do not call myself a Christian (keeping the ideal free), but I can make it obvious that the others are even less so.'[26]

The last straw – for others as well as Kierkegaard – had been that the revered Mynster had also been described as being less so.

His demotion was one that the perceptive primate would without doubt have seen implied in that subversive category of the single individual. Although a Lutheran with pietistic leanings might be expected to embrace such a category, Kierkegaard's insistence on the single individual's being 'alone, in the whole world alone, alone face to face with God' left no room for a high command.[27] It is indeed polemical, but the category only leaves openings for the foot soldier who already knows what the contest is about and how to engage in it. If, in the end, the primate of the Danish Church did not understand that he was in the line of fire too, then perhaps it was up to Kierkegaard to put his own life on the line. Dying would also be a way of convincing others and himself that it had not all been vanity and indulgence, or just a way of excusing his own transgressions. Reaching back to the charged and convicted master-thief, Kierkegaard appears to have looked on his own death as something that could help others to see that it was his opponents who were in the wrong. If not, his literal 'annihilation' as an authority would show that his own conviction in another sense was real enough.

## 10

# Death and its Impact

The final entry, dated 25 September 1855, in Kierkegaard's last journal opens by saying, 'Our destiny in this life is to be brought to the highest pitch of world-weariness.'[1] Is this the dismal result of his self-scripted education? Or was it more like a personal premonition? The date of the entry was that of *The Moment*'s last published issue. The pamphlet had caused a furore that could have given Kierkegaard a sense of being engaged in open combat. He was again 'in character' as a newspaper combatant, as he had been when he started his career twenty years earlier under a tentative pseudonym.

Those who knew him thought he was bearing the strain well. He may even have been rather enjoying letting off steam and noting who would be scalded by the heat. Accompanying him to his new home in Klædeboderne, Hans Brøchner was surprised that Kierkegaard managed to retain 'not just his usual equanimity and cheerfulness but even his sense of humour'.[2] But this would be their last meeting. On 2 October, just a week after the publication of the ninth issue of *The Moment*, Kierkegaard collapsed in the street. He was taken by carriage first to his home and then at his own request to Frederik's Hospital. There his condition steadily worsened, and six weeks later he died.

During those weeks, he received frequent visits from his solicitous friend and confidant Emil Boesen, now tending a congregation at Horsens in eastern Jutland. Boesen's record of their conversations leaves an impression of a world-weary man coming to terms with his past. Kierkegaard had preached enough about having to die *to* the world, in the sense of seeing beyond the finite goals we set ourselves in escaping questions of what we are doing here at all. He had written his way to an answer that accorded with his basic instincts about God and faith, but now those answers too must face him in the form of a question. If they didn't, then Boesen did it for him. When he asked Kierkegaard if he could pray in peace, the answer was

> Yes, I can; then I pray first for the forgiveness of sins, that everything may be forgiven; then I pray to be free of despair at the time of my death, and the saying frequently occurs to me that death must be well pleasing to God; and then I pray for what I would so much like to be the case, that I know a little in advance when death occurs.

It was fine and sunny outside, and Boesen said, 'When you sit and talk like that you seem healthy enough just to get up and leave with me.' Kierkegaard replied,

> Yes, there's just one problem. I can't walk. But then there's another means of transport: I can be lifted up. I have had a feeling of becoming an angel, getting wings, that too is what's going to happen, sitting astride a cloud and singing Hallelujah, Hallelujah, Hallelujah! I know any idiot can say that; it all depends on how it is said.[3]

The ironist too was still alive. Boesen asked if all that was because he believed and took refuge in God's mercy through Christ. Kierkegaard's reply was, 'Yes, of course, what else?' Would he want to have changed anything he had said? Had he not, after all, expressed himself in unreal and strict terms? His response was, 'That is how it should be; otherwise it doesn't help. What good would it do first to speak for awakening and then for appeasement? Why do you bother me with this?' On a previous occasion, Boesen had found Kierkegaard very weak, but after a while he asked him if there was anything he wanted to say.

No; yes, greet everyone, I've been very fond of them all, and tell them my life is a great, to others unknown and incomprehensible, suffering. It all looked like pride and vanity but wasn't. I am not at all better than others, I have said that and never anything else. I had my thorn in the flesh, and therefore did not marry and was unable to take on an official position. I am after all a theology graduate, and had a public title and private favour: I could have got what I wanted, but I became the exception instead. The day went in work and excitement and in the evening I am put aside; out of the way – it was the exception.

It was 'all right', he said, as 'one who lived as an exception' to 'die within the category of the universal'.

Two weeks before collapsing in the street, the same had happened at a party given by Israel Levin, the friend and assistant who had helped with several chores, including taking manuscripts to the printer and proofreading *The Sickness Unto Death*. As Levin records,

He was sitting on the sofa and had been so gay, amusing, and charming, and then he slid from the sofa to the floor; we helped him up, but he stammered: 'O-h-h, j-j-just leave it t-t-till the m-maid sweeps it out in the morning', and fainted shortly afterwards.[4]

When the maid had swept out the body, would the spirit go marching on? Or is 'spirit' only something we aspire to be in a world that we 'die to' enough to engage in what Kierkegaard called works of love? He opposed ascetic withdrawal of the kind advocated by Schopenhauer, a writer he had recently come across and, despite 'total disagreement', admired as 'superbly unparalleled' in his 'well-aimed abuse'. Schopenhauer's was the kind of invective that was needed against the 'priests of religion' when 'Christendom is everywhere in such a state of degradation and demoralization that by comparison paganism is divine elevation.'[5] As was typical of him, Kierkegaard noted that he, Søren Aabye (SA), and Arthur Schopenhauer (AS) were 'no doubt inversely related'.

As for being 'fond of them all', if there were no decided exceptions, there were certainly qualifications. Visits were unwelcome, other than those from this one confidant who could grasp his confessions. Not even his long-term friend and assistant Jens Giødwad was allowed in. It was understandable given his condition. But when Peter Christian heard of his brother's worsening condition and came to the hospital, Søren had the duty nurse turn him away. Peter had to travel the long way back to his parsonage with his mission unaccomplished.

It was a sad ending to a lifelong conflict of personalities that had peaked in an extemporized address to the Roskilde Convention. Peter had praised Martensen's work as a model of composure compared to Søren's 'ecstasy'. Remarking bitterly in his journal that, in comparison with Martensen even in his most sober moments, St Paul himself would be pure ecstasy, Kierkegaard said that what saddened him was that, in the absence of any other public reaction to his latest work, it was his brother who came out with 'a pretty good idea of what it is all about'.[6] It was this nod-and-wink confiding in public that led Søren in private to describe Peter as a 'fuddy-duddy', 'devoid of ideas', a 'vapid gadabout' and a 'front figure of mediocrity'.[7] The disappointed Peter had, of course, been hoping for a last-minute reconciliation.

Boesen came to the hospital a little later on the day that Peter was denied an audience. Asked if anything could be done to repair the breach, Kierkegaard said it required action not words, and he had acted. On that same occasion, Boesen asked him whether he would like to receive the last rites. 'Yes, indeed,' replied Kierkegaard, 'but from a layman, not a pastor.' When Boesen said this would be difficult, Kierkegaard said, 'Then I'll do without.' Boesen responded that it would not be right, to which Kierkegaard replied, 'The matter is not in debate, I have made up my mind, my choice is made. The priests are royal functionaries, royal functionaries have nothing to do with Christianity.'

On an early visit, when Boesen had found his friend in low spirits, Kierkegaard spoke of Regine. He said that what went wrong with Regine was that his life and fate had become that of an extraordinary emissary; he was under the control of Governance:

> I'd thought it could be changed but it couldn't, then I dissolved
> the relationship. How odd, the husband became Governor,
> I don't like it . . . it would have been better if it had ended
> quietly. It was right that she got Schlegel, that was the first
> understanding and then I came along and disturbed things.
> She suffered a great deal with me . . .

Boesen then said, though without recording the words, that Kierkegaard spoke of her 'with great affection and sadness'. He could, however, report a final spark of humour: 'I was afraid she would become a governess, and now she is one in the West Indies.'

We might guess that, if only it had ended quietly without Schlegel's disturbance, Kierkegaard could have kept Regine to himself and have her forever associated with his life work, dedicated as the discourses had been from the start to this 'dear reader'. Towards the end, Boesen reproached Kierkegaard for not having visited him in Horsens. The reply came, 'No, how could I find time for that!'

The last time Emil Boesen saw him, Kierkegaard could scarcely talk. Boesen had to leave town to tend to his flock, and Søren Aabye

Kierkegaard died soon after. The official diagnosis was 'paraplegia', or bilateral immobility, but the root cause was set down tentatively as tuberculosis. Later investigations suggest an 'ascending spinal paralysis', a neurological ailment whose causes are still unknown.

At his brother's prompting, the funeral service, on 18 November 1855, was conducted at the Church of Our Lady by the archdeacon E. C. Tryde. Hans Christian Andersen was present and gives a vivid description:

> Søren Kierkegaard was buried last Sunday, following a service at the Church of Our Lady, where the parties concerned had done very little. The church pews were closed and the aisles unusually crowded. Ladies in red and blue hast were coming and going; ditto dogs with muzzles. At the grave-site itself there was a scandal: when the ceremony *there* [at Assistens Graveyard] was over (that is when Tryde had cast earth upon the coffin), a son of a sister of the deceased stepped forward and denounced the fact that he had been buried in this fashion. He declared – and this was his point more or less – that Søren Kierkegaard had resigned from our society, and therefore we ought not to bury him in accordance with our customs! I was not out there, but it was said to have been unpleasant. The newspapers say little about it. In last Thursday's number of *Fædrelandet* this nephew has published his speech along with some afterthoughts. To me the entire affair is a distorted picture of Søren K.: I don't understand it![8]

Perhaps what Andersen found distorted was a Kierkegaard presented as so much an outsider as to have placed himself beyond his own society's church. This was the same Kierkegaard who, until quite recently, had been listening attentively to Mynster's sermons every Sunday.

Always a warm admirer of his uncle, the nephew in question was Henrik Lund, the young man who had once sent a copy of *Either/Or* to his other uncle in Brazil. After serving as a physician in the Schleswig War that lasted from 1848 to 1851, and not long after graduating, he had helped to transcribe material for a draft of 'On My Activity as an Author', which had been published in August 1851. Both Henrik and his physician brother Michael had attended their dying uncle at Frederik's Hospital. Later, when Kierkegaard's books came up for auction, Henrik was an eager bidder.[9]

Henrik could affirm in his graveside speech that, over the years, he had become bound to his uncle 'by ties of friendship as well as blood'. *The Moment* was still ringing in his ears. Quoting the passage about 'our all being Christians', he pointed out that in no other religious society would someone who had 'left it so decisively', and 'with no prior recantation', nevertheless be 'looked upon after his death as a member of that society'. Unadvisedly, he also suggested that the church had taken over the proceedings for the money, but he also directed a jibe at another uncle: Peter Christian had arranged this to save the family's reputation. Described by onlookers as 'a young physician' and 'visibly upset' with 'a New Testament in his hand', Henrik ended by saying, 'I have spoken and freed my spirit!'[10]

Martensen's spirit, on the other hand, was burdened. That a 'large cortège of mourners (in full pomp, what irony!)' had followed the coffin was bad enough, but that it was mainly made up of the young and 'a mass of obscure personages', with 'not a single dignitary among them', clearly dismayed the new primate.[11] Was that annoying man on the way to martyrdom? Whether or not the thought crossed Martensen's mind, one reason for a show of strength on the part of the 'people' was a cholera epidemic that had hit Copenhagen in the late summer of 1853. It revealed scandalous deficiencies in the city's hygiene and welfare apparatus. Thousands among the lower classes died. In Denmark, the better-off citizens spent their summer vacations out of town. The fact that, with few exceptions, the clergy too found it convenient to be on vacation at the time aroused deep indignation among the poorer people and those concerned with their welfare. When Kierkegaard's attack on the Church came, the mood in many quarters in which *The Moment* was unknown had been receptive, and a wider stage was set for the conflict to come.

It was this, above all, that scandalized Martensen when word of the graveside irregularity – that a nephew had waved both the New Testament and *The Moment* in claiming to be a witness to the truth that the Church was burying Kierkegaard for the money – had reached him and was not to be taken quietly. Against the advice of the archdeacon, who thought the matter should be allowed to rest, Martensen decided that the future of the established church was at stake. The affair ended in Copenhagen's criminal court, where the prosecutor subsequently demanded a prison sentence. Henrik was let off with a hundred rix-dollar fine to be paid to Copenhagen's poor relief. He subsequently spent some time in a mental hospital and was treated for an unspecified 'nervous complaint'.

Since Henrik was an attending physician, and in the absence of any other obvious candidate, Kierkegaard had asked Henrik on his deathbed to look after his estate when he died. So it was Henrik who sent off to the Danish Virgin Islands what letters, books and other items Kierkegaard wished Regine to have. And it was Henrik who began arranging the enormous store of journals and manuscripts, though he soon found it too much of a job. Like so many closely involved with Kierkegaard – P. L. Møller, Goldschmidt, Fritz Schlegel and Regine – Henrik too sought sanctuary abroad: in fact, he settled in the Virgin Islands to work as a physician on St John, and thus for a year or two, he was a virtual neighbour of the Schlegels on St Croix. He also returned to Copenhagen in 1860, the same year the Schlegels did.

Peter Kierkegaard was able to inform the still-exiled Schlegels that his brother had made Regine his sole legatee, on the grounds that for Søren, an engagement was as binding as a marriage. When

Fritz learned this, and after consulting Regine, he wrote to say that they could not accept this most unusual bequest.

One sad ending to the conflict between Peter and Søren had been the latter's deathbed refusal to talk to his brother. Another would be Peter's own fate. Like his father, he lived to be 82, but thirteen years before his death, when he was bishop of Aalborg in north Jutland, he resigned his civil rights and placed himself in legal custody. Peter Christian Kierkegaard had become mentally disabled. Although the manuscript of the eulogy at his brother's funeral was lost, when asked 26 years later if he could remember any of it, the bishop recalled that he had spoken of his remorse at not realizing that his brother's vision had 'become partially darkened and distorted from exertions and suffering in the heat of battle, causing his blows to fall wildly and blindly'. He had regretted not having 'enticed' or 'compelled' Søren with the 'confident gaze and the mild embraces of love' to take 'a long and quiet rest'. The wild blows mentioned by Peter Christian were explicitly an allusion to a Norwegian saga in which they were dealt by one Ølver, a man whose heroic deeds were suspected of being performed while he was drunk and whose full name (Ølvir miklimunr) means 'bigmouth'. The knowledgeable among his listeners would understand that Søren was out of his mind and had no control over his words.[12] The poignancy of Peter's recollection lies less in the infidelity of an elder brother saying in public that his younger brother had lost his mind, than in the distinct possibility that the recollection was instrumental in his losing his own. He had tried to make amends. In 1859 Peter Christian published *The Point of View for My Work as an Author*, and he arranged for the republication of *Edifying Discourses in Various Spirits* in 1862, the first edition to become sold out.

Peter Christian would live long enough to learn the hard truth that the Kierkegaard name would now forever be associated with that of the sickly Søren. The fact that by the mid-1870s Kierkegaard's first biographer Georg Brandes felt the need to 'explain' the phenomenon speaks volumes for the demonic facility with which this self-appointed custodian of Christianity could cause tremors in the world of literature and, more widely – or perhaps 'deeply' – in those of philosophy and religion. Brandes's Danish biography was published simultaneously in Swedish and soon after in German in Scandinavia, and later on the European continent. Kierkegaard's influence could be felt in the plays of Henrik Ibsen, who – like so many others – had procured a copy of *Either/Or.* It was a book about which – on its first appearance – Hans Christian Andersen could inform his friend Signe Læssøe down in Paris that a 'new literary comet . . . has soared in the heavens here –

> a harbinger and a bringer of bad fortune. It is so demonic that one reads and reads it, puts it aside in dissatisfaction, but always picks it up again, because one can neither let it go nor hold onto it . . . You have no idea what a sensation it has caused. I think that no book has caused such a stir with the reading public since Rousseau placed his *Confessions* on the altar. After one has read it, one feels disgust for the author, but one profoundly recognizes his intelligence and his talent.[13]

# 11

# In Time's Centrifuge

The intelligence and talent are still celebrated. Disgust, once not
infrequent, now comes as a surprise and when present, is usually
assisted by the graphic rhetoric of a caricature. The grimace of
caricature can overprint our access to the person. The author
of a biography decorated with a caricatured portrait 'from
memory' that has become a staple introduction to Kierkegaard's
person can talk of a 'twisted life'.[1] Another commentator sees 'the
spindly figure with the umbrella' in every pseudonym: we read of
a 'hypochondriacal young man born old, with his eccentricities',
and of his love affair that 'we are sick of hearing about . . . [and] his
abysmal melancholia'. Topping this bill, yet another commentator
tells of the 'desperate attempts of a misshapen man . . . for who . . .
the desire not to know the truth was an important element in . . .
his faith'.[2]

The surprise here is to read such words from Anglophone
writers whose most likely source has been the largely successful
missionary work of a confessed Kierkegaard 'promoter'. It was in
the late 1930s and early '40s that Walter Lowrie's translations and
biographies first brought Kierkegaard's work to a wide Anglophone
audience. It was also he who started the still-widespread habit of
referring companionably to a writer who had written very little to
his own contemporaries' taste as 'S.K.' The Kierkegaard launched
by this promoter bore so little resemblance to the polemicist that
one wonders how a writer whose burden of melancholy, his thorn

in the flesh, and who was able to goad Golden Age Denmark's sensibilities so intensely, could receive such an enthusiastic response elsewhere.[3] Could the times have caught up with Kierkegaard and given him, at last, his true audience? Certainly readers versed in existentialist ways of thought would be better tuned in to his concerns. Or was there something special about Denmark at the time, something we have escaped, that made his countrymen especially vulnerable to his polemic?

No doubt something can be said for both, but in the present context, it is worth dwelling for a moment on the latter. As a thriving trading nation with its West Indian colonies, with artists among the best in Europe and gifted writers in a time when literary art had high prestige, Denmark was then enjoying an upward curve that expunged the memories and consequences of having sided with Napoleon. Perhaps the fact that Copenhagen was a smallish town helped to bring about this self-advertised outsider. The reviewer of a recent biography wonders whether Kierkegaard would have 'found his existence so absorbingly important' had he been born in a larger city where 'the edges of his ego might have frayed into the general fabric of indifference'.[4] It is a good enough question but as hard to answer as 'What agonies could have been averted if the young Adolf Hitler had received more encouragement as a budding artist?' Contexts supply the occasion, but the active ingredient in the outcome is, in our case, and as a commentator nicely puts it, the fact that a 'sensitive, sulky, ironical and precocious child' had both the temperament required for the 'later burgeoning of genius' and an ability to 'find his feet' when the 'ground fell away beneath him'.[5] Søren Aabye Kierkegaard was bound to be a spoke in the wheels of his society. In person as well as word, he was an archetype of the *à rebours* mentality iconized later by Huysmans and, in that sense at least, a forerunner of what was to come. The drooping statue outside the Royal Library with an introspective seated Kierkegaard would be conspicuously out of place among the inspiringly erect Neoclassical works lending their air of perfection to Copenhagen's Thorvaldsen Museum.

Kierkegaard arrived in the USA as an intriguing cultural import from abroad to be embraced or reviled 'in abstracto', as Kierkegaard would say. Here was an author much of whose writing seemed prescient of something in the air and whose views on religion would in any case heat up some tepid theological discussion, perhaps even give pause to some whose faith tended to the habitual. The caricature too, which came with the package, could be looked on in a spirit of pity and even affection, except by those whose immediate reaction was scorn or disgust. That overworked, stooped figure may have come off the rails somewhat towards the end, but there is still much to learn and, most of all, to 'discuss'.

Yes, discuss. The centrifuge of time has whipped up a veritable storm of 'Kierkegaard discussion' and has provided thousands more livelihoods than the one thousand or so livings upon which Kierkegaard poured his scorn. That many, or even a majority, of these discussions revolve around Christian concepts that Kierkegaard found 'fossilized' invites some hard questions. Does this interest in Kierkegaard take serious account of his criticisms of the Lutheran Church as he knew it, or was his criticism at fault? Or is it that discussions, conducted by academics among themselves, can set these criticisms aside and take them to be among the things that can be interestingly discussed?

That question applies primarily in the case of the edifying and Christian discourses, generally taken to represent Kierkegaard's fresh insights into how the Christian concepts *should* enter our lives: in single-mindedness, forthrightness, open-heartedness, optimism and even joyfulness. The question is then, what more is there to say about these? Are we to approach them with the aim of improving on them, or are we getting closer to his meaning by clarifying in a more perspicuous vocabulary what Kierkegaard wrote in a deliberately 'unscholarly' style?

Another question is, are we in the right forum? Yet another is, is any *forum* the right place to be in? The answer depends on how great our interest is in the motivation behind these signed religious publications, and on how seriously we take Kierkegaard's claims in this respect. By ascribing a sufficient degree of schizophrenia to his intentions as a writer, we can interpret the high-minded discourses purely as a demonstration of Kierkegaard's preferred self-image as a religious writer. He writes in a tone higher than most to show that he was something more than a writer of dark romance or even sleaze. Alternatively, the discourses and deliberations can be read independently of the pseudonyms as contributions to a general clarification of what Kierkegaard takes to be the key concepts for Christian faith. The thought here is that if he were alive today, he might wish that a more sophisticated analytical apparatus had been available to him. He might thank us for finishing the job for him by clarifying and even cleaning up his concepts.

The focus of this biography has tended to weaken any such sense of authorial schizophrenia. It is, of course, a matter of choice how one reads Kierkegaard. What Kierkegaard himself believed posterity would primarily be interested in was 'not only my writings but indeed my life, the intriguing secret of the whole machinery'.[6] It was the way in which the working parts had been geared to the task of becoming his actively unified self that he believed would engross us. His own reconstructions on what it was 'all about' can be, and generally have been, exposed to programmatic suspicion. But if, as it is fair to conjecture, Kierkegaard was actually engaged from the outset on the 'domestic journey' announced in that somewhat mysterious letter, then it is more than likely that the topics of the discourses and deliberation relate to items or events in that journey's itinerary. Though the majority of these were dedicated to Regine, they were also written for himself in continuation of a search for a unifying principle that, as it soon turned out, would have to take account of his own bad conscience. Take the discourse

'Purity of Heart is to Will One Thing', the first of three published in 1847 as *Edifying Discourses in Various Spirits* (also translated as 'Edifying Addresses of Varying Tenor'). As the other discourses are, this one is based on a quotation from the Bible: in this case, the author is the Apostle James, in whose Epistle (James 4:8), we read, 'Draw nigh to God and he will draw nigh to you. Cleanse your hands, ye sinners; and purify your hearts ye double-minded.' The three sections of this discourse tell the reader that in order properly to will one thing 'in the true sense', you must be 'willing' the Good, but that the Good can only be willed if in doing so you are not aiming to achieve some worldly end, for instance escaping punishment for not doing so. Furthermore, you have to be 'willing' everything for the Good, and that means that *all* your worldly aims must be directed at the Good, while willing to do *everything* for the Good includes suffering for it, something that may include losing your life. It may sound like a formula for the life of Jesus, but with *Practice in Christianity* just round the corner, telling us to take Christ as our exemplar, it may be just what it is.

Is there then any point in trying to come up with a more amenable version that might find a place in our own ideas of a moral world? In the biblical context of these discourses, the notion is clear enough and entirely in keeping with Kierkegaard's seminal project. Removing the latter from that context gives it quite another complexion and introduces questions that Kierkegaard would no doubt have felt unnecessary to raise. That the discourse was at least not something he took lightly is shown by the efforts he took in bringing this discourse into a form that he found suitable. All three discourses occupied him from May 1846 to January 1847.

Except for special groups of writers and intellectuals (notably the 'Inklings' in England, with whom Lowrie was associated), Kierkegaard was for a time cultivated in the Anglophone world almost exclusively in conclaves of those who saw something in the texts to their taste or, through them, something in the author with

A caricature sketch of Kierkegaard by Wilhelm Marstrand (1810–1873).

which they could identify. Gradually, as Kierkegaard gained in academic respectability, 'societies' and 'associations' found places on the itineraries of philosophical and theological conferences, eventually merging seamlessly into their main agendas. Some refocusing would be needed if it had not already been done. Philosophers in particular had to cherry-pick to find topics suitable for their accredited fora, but when the door was opened for career opportunities, Kierkegaard became academic business as usual. Today his relevance for academic discussion in many areas is taken for granted.

The predictable result has been a drift away from the man and his motivation towards the wide spectrum of topics that touch on his authorial adventure. It may be something that Kierkegaard anticipated, but for his immediate future it was not something he wished. An explicit reason for shunning debate was precisely that he feared that his work might become an object of 'interest', or himself become, as he says, a 'phenomenon in the world'.[7] It was as a 'phenomenon' that Brandes would market Kierkegaard but also explain him. The literary theorists would be the first to lose sight of the drift or to try to slot it into history. In whatever way theorists would deal with Kierkegaard's work, their mood and attitude would only show that they had misunderstood, or else that if they did understand, they acknowledged their disinterest in the polemic. If Kierkegaard's 'interest' had been *in* the writing, the only other relevant interest he would anticipate was a living appreciation of its trajectory.

Naturally, the expectation if real was naive. However, it was as his authorship neared its close that he saw his polemic reaching its pitch. His concern would be to avoid the attentions of those, like P. L. Møller, who saw an unbalanced author at work, or those who listened to his brother and although prepared to read all that was eminently readable, would dismiss or ignore everything that had been compressed into the 'category of the single individual'.

The last piece in the final published number of *The Moment* includes the following complaint to the clergy:

> Proof and refutation in one! The proof of Christianity's truth being that people have risked everything for it, is refuted or made suspect by the priest in delivering the proof doing the exact opposite . . .[8]

Taking him at his word, the remark is one into which the whole authorship can be read. Those who come with a proof of their faith have not only been wasting their time, and now also his; they are 'proving' that they have no faith. If someone were to begin questioning Kierkegaard about something he had written and began, 'Look here, Kierkegaard, is it quite true that . . .' or, 'Søren, that's an interesting point about . . .' or, 'I myself think Hegel did quite a good job making pantheism respectable', we might imagine him saying,

Sorry it's not me, it's the pseudonyms, or if you are thinking of that discourse on what it is to 'will one thing', then you must either take it or leave it as it is. It's the way I read the New Testament. But in general, as I've tried to make clear from the start in my prefaces and postscripts, I am not here to argue with you, or even make things clearer than I have tried to make them. All of it is an effort to show what it was for me to spend a life of writing in the spirit of someone willing to live and die for an idea. That is what I said even before I began and discovered I could do this. It was what I had to do in order to pull myself together and stay sane. If you have the same problem, though I believe nowadays people call it 'issue', then try it yourself. As for my after-life, I see they've just published a collection called *Kierkegaard and Political Theory: Religion, Aesthetics, Politics and the Intervention of the Single Individual*. Maybe [the irony breaking through] you can have a look at it for me and tell me what I think.

From its autobiographical perspective, Kierkegaard's writing was a risky business; it was a venture that he followed through to the end. In terms familiar to analytical philosophers as well as existentialists, it was a 'personal project', a project of the kind that Sartre calls 'basic' because it is self-defining for the one who undertakes it. Whatever may be missing by default from his own true self-image, if ever someone was self-defining as an author, it was Kierkegaard. Although the writing was a 'cure', he was not one to lose sight of the ailment while taking the remedy.[9] Even if he is diagnosed as a compulsive polemicist who enjoyed presenting his contemporaries with standards he knew they could never meet, this does not in itself license the removal of the cure-seeking author from the unruly equation of the evolving *opus*. Nor, without the professed proviso that they are transplants, does it give a go-ahead for plucking out texts or their themes for seminar topics. Converting an ongoing risky business into 'stills' to be extracted and examined *in vitro* in a wider context is itself a risky business; it removes what Kierkegaard calls the 'sting of the decision in action'.[10]

It also induces partial myopia, making it harder to distinguish what of Kierkegaard and what of themselves his admirers and critics write into their appraisals. In wondering what Kierkegaard might make of it all were he to witness academic discussion of his work, we might think of a similar case. Aircraftman Shaw, alias Colonel T. E. Lawrence, was wont out of sheer curiosity to sneak in on the American war correspondent Lowell Thomas's public lectures, illustrated by film clips of the deeds of Lawrence of Arabia, listening there unrecognized but also not recognizing himself, yet with an oddly detached mixture of shame and a not-altogether-vicarious pride.

Kierkegaard is explicit about his writings not being intended *for* debate. Nor are they written in a way that *invites* it. Whatever their literary appeal, the discourses are more readily absorbed by those able to appreciate their moral challenge. The *Point of View* tells history that the dialectical Johannes Climacus is jockeying readers 'back' from the 'System' to a proper grasp of the place of religion – namely, in 'inwardness' – while his colleagues in the early pseudonymity are coaxing readers away from their 'aesthetic' distortions of religion to a living appreciation.[11] Of course, to any sceptical and even just wary mind, *The Point of View*'s explanations can themselves appear distorted or even delusionary. A commentator talks of Kierkegaard taking 'charge' of his own 'posthumous reputation'.[12] Apart from lacking any finer distinctions, such claims are, of course, hard to refute, but equally hard to justify. One may as well speculate that Kierkegaard looked to his own reputation only to ensure Regine's. The less dramatic conclusion that he was trying to be honest can be backed only by appeal to other claims harder to call in question – as, for instance, where the same commentator concedes that 'only a cynic' can doubt the 'emotional authenticity' of Kierkegaard's expression of his sense of God's love.[13] Kierkegaard later admitted that in a time of intense pressure, some 'poetic creativity' had crept into his journal entries, but then he added disarmingly that it happened 'whenever I pick up my pen'. In the same place, however, he claims that 'in [his] inner being', he is 'quite otherwise concise and clear about [him]self'.[14] Should we take that too as a creative slip of the pen?

The image presented by the Kierkegaard who became staple fare in North America differs sharply from that of the writer embraced by a new wave of European philosophers bent on calling into question the assumptions of 'modernity'. The rise of phenomenology helped with its renewal and revision of Descartes' focus on the individual's experience. Himself a doctor of divinity and sometime pastor, Walter Lowrie had spent time in Germany and Italy, but also in Switzerland, where his first encounter with Kierkegaard was through the Swiss theologian Karl Barth. Rejecting 'natural' theology, with its assumption that God and his creatures have something in common, Barth had said that *if* he had a system, it was a minimal one that limited itself to Kierkegaard's radical distinction between time and eternity. Where German and French receptions of Kierkegaard clearly favoured secular readings, Lowrie, as his priorities in translating clearly show, saw it as his mission to prevent this happening to his fellow countrymen. He began with the later 'Christian' discourses and the posthumously published *Point of View*, though with none of Kierkegaard's qualms about publishing that 'report to history' to his own contemporaries. Lowrie's dedicated salesmanship came close to preaching.

Europeans were selective in the other direction. Brandes, in his biography from 1877, had softened the seemingly hard religious 'premise' in Kierkegaard's work by reading the later works (*Practice in Christianity*, in particular) as inspirational rather than instructive.[15] Propagandizing on behalf of a Kierkegaard less obsessed by the need for pain and suffering, he wrote to Nietzsche saying that Kierkegaard was 'one of the profoundest psychologists to be met with anywhere'.[16] On the brink of insanity, Nietzsche could not respond, but other Europeans found Kierkegaard for themselves. Left-wing post-Hegelians were especially receptive. Georg Lukács, the Hungarian literary theorist, encountered Kierkegaard through the German sociologist and polymath Max Weber, noted for his diagnoses of social change and 'disenchantment' with religion. His prophecy that in a 'rationalizing' world there would be increasing individualization was anticipated by Kierkegaard, who saw it on the contrary as a means to seeing what religion and Christianity really are. A qualified admirer in his young days, Lukács had criticized Kierkegaard for making a poem out of his life, but when Kierkegaard's name became associated with existentialism ('that permanent carnival of fetishized inwardness'), he became wholly critical.[17] The cult of subjectivity belonged to the bourgeoisie and, as a Marxist Hegelian, Lukács regarded any talk of the eternal as a way of sanitizing a self outside the continual though progressive flux of history. A similar criticism came from Herbert Marcuse, whose generous claim that Kierkegaard's work was 'the last great attempt to restore religion as the ultimate organon for liberating humanity from the destructive impact of an oppressive social order' has rather more Marcuse in it than Kierkegaard.[18]

Although Simone de Beauvoir records that Kierkegaard was eagerly read in their circle, Jean-Paul Sartre claims not to have been influenced. He seems nevertheless to have felt a challenge. Although 'we cannot revive the martyr of inwardness' in our day and age, there is still the *writer* who addressed personal themes existentially and with a contagious 'potency' and 'virulence'.[19] Not so much a legacy, in other words, as an example. If Kierkegaard has something to offer outside a specifically religious context, for Sartre it is that he has 'revealed [that] each man' is all mankind as 'the singular universal'.[20]

Martin Heidegger also found Kierkegaard's insights congenial. The characteristics he ascribes to the 'averageness' of *Das Man* (often translated as 'the they', though lexically identical with the Danish *man*, normally translated as 'one', as in 'what one does') follow Kierkegaard's own examples of 'levelling' so closely that we can easily picture a well-thumbed copy of *Eine literarsch Anziege* on the desk in Heidegger's Black Forest cabin. In acknowledging his debt to 'S. Kierkegaard', however, Heidegger finds Kierkegaard's treatment of the *Existenzproblem als existenzielles* too constricted by its Hegelian framework.[21] He imported Kierkegaard's 'anxiety' and 'guilt' into his *Daseinanalyse,* but Kierkegaard's seminal account in *The Concept of Anxiety* is 'psychological' and has a 'theological' focus (on original sin).[22] Heidegger does not see that work as a brick in a literary edifice intended by Kierkegaard to cast a deeper shadow over that Hegelian framework.

Heidegger, more than Sartre, was open to the sense of a fundamental human need for fulfilment of the kind that something we call 'religion' appeals to. It may be that Sartre's 'singular universal' is too bland a category to capture the basic human situation, even when confined to time. It has indeed been said of Sartre that he retained the office of God but appointed Man as his deputy. Recently, Jürgen Habermas, a later representative of the Marx-inspired Frankfurt School to which Marcuse belonged, and similarly dedicated to secular reasoning, has dared to herald a 'post-secular' age, seeing it as one in which Kierkegaardian faith can be restored as a valuable resource in political debate on public issues, even though these themselves are still to be conducted in purely secular terms.[23] So, yes, 'martyrdom' may be a contingent and psychologically explicable aspect of Kierkegaard's own 'basic project'; but in the form of the 'quiet hours' of a reflecting politician's mind, his 'inwardness' can still have a place in worldly affairs.

Much excellent scholarship has helped us to grasp texts whose allusions are not only from the past but often local in their references. It takes time to find out that Kierkegaard's ethics is largely Aristotelian rather than Kantian, although at first it can look like the latter. On the other hand, readers innocent of the distinction might come to the same result themselves without the need to place it in terms minted for their special purposes by philosophers. As the perceptive psychologist that he was, Kierkegaard may well have anticipated questions that critical readers were to raise in the future. Some have been mentioned here. In writing *Either/Or*, was he creatively doodling on vast envelopes in which he could enclose secret signals to Regine? Were the guilt and the penance the main thing and this huge literary spin-off just a perquisite, though one that gave him an audience and the self-confirmation of its response? Or were the works themselves the whole point, since writing was what kept him from falling apart? Did it really 'educate' him and make him what he became? Did he really owe his talent to God and its discovery to Regine? When Kierkegaard asked himself what it really enabled him to achieve, would the answer have to be that it gave him satisfying scope for an inveterate urge to polemicize but at the same time a chance to defend his father's faith against all comers? Or was it all, after all, as he knew someone would be bound to ask, just a substitute for a marriage that his physical condition and all-too-busy mind would prevent him from consummating? But having asked the questions, we can ask another: what is the point? They are questions of the kind we can ask about ourselves on whatever scale. Posing them helps to penetrate the facades and caricatures.

Slight, thin and delicate, denied practically all the physical conditions which, compared with others, could qualify me, too, as a whole human being; melancholy, sick in my mind, profoundly and inwardly a failure in many ways, I was given one thing: an eminently astute mind, presumably to keep me from being completely defenceless . . .[24]

So speaks the man himself. In recorded memories of the actual Kierkegaard, he is almost always 'little'. His teacher Professor Sibbern spoke of that 'witty, somewhat sarcastic face' and a 'brisk way of walking' but added that he 'never knew him to be melancholic'.[25] Although, on first seeing him, Hans Brøchner took Kierkegaard to be a draper's assistant, doubtless thinking of the father's trade, as they began speaking, he 'realized he belonged somewhere else than behind a counter with a measuring tape'. He adds that there was something 'very irregular in his whole appearance', and, with his hair standing on end in a 'rumpled mass almost six inches over his forehead', Kierkegaard had a 'strange confused look'.[26] Meïr Aron Goldschmidt, editor of the *Corsair*, records from about that time a 'fresh complexion' but a young man who was 'thin' and with his shoulders 'a little hunched forward, his eyes intelligent, lively, and superior with a mixture of good nature and malice'.[27] Goldschmidt later also gave the following description:

He looked like a person who was elevated above many or most of the ordinary conditions and temptations of life, though not in such a way that he seemed enviable or happy . . . He went about like a thought that had got distracted at the very moment it was formed.[28]

The poet Henrik Hertz, who, in commenting on the style of Kierkegaard's first book *From the Papers of One Still Living*, had declared that 'the Mesopotamian language is a strange language', describes Kierkegaard as of

Photograph of plaster model of the bronze statue by Louis Hasselriis (1844–1912) in front of the Royal Library.

middle height, with broad shoulders and a rather rounded back, a thin lower body; a bit bent over when he walks; thin, rather long hair; blue? eyes; the voice often breaking into a treble or a bit piping. Also quite easily provoked to laughter, but suddenly switching to seriousness. There was something pleasing about him, not so much the promise of anything special as many different things . . . something entertaining.[29]

Brøchner again recalled 'something infinitely loving and gentle in his eye', and he described Kierkegaard as a man of 'friendly good will', with the 'gentle and loving side' increasingly outweighing the 'strongly ironic and polemical element that was in him by nature'.[30] At the time of the break and in the wake of the 'deception', when Regine's elder brother Jonas had sent Kierkegaard a note saying that he 'had taught him to hate as no one had hated before', the elder sister, Cornelia, in whom Kierkegaard saw a 'rare and genuine womanliness', said that although she could not understand 'Magister Kierkegaard', she 'nevertheless believed he was a good man'.[31]

In her old age and after eight years of widowhood in which she had ample time to let the now-famous Kierkegaard once more invade her heart, Regine Schlegel could stick to externals when asked by a younger friend if a portrait in a recently published *History of Literature* resembled her one-time fiancé. Her diplomatic answer was: 'Both yes and no, Kierkegaard's exterior was easy to caricature and people exploited that.' As for his always being presented as stiff-backed, Regine replied, 'Yes, he was somewhat high-shouldered and his head tilted forward a bit, probably from all the reading and writing at his desks.'[32]

The statue outside the Royal Library in Copenhagen, with the head tilted slightly forward, whether or not a true likeness, provides a refreshing corrective to our usual visual contact with this unusual man, who, although more than sufficiently aware of his talents, died quite unsuspecting of the profusion and confusion of interests his literary cure for melancholia would attract. Had he known how much he would come to be read by so many, we may imagine his better nature suppressing malice enough – and perhaps even irony, although that may be asking too much – to light up his face with the ghost of a sarcastic smile as if to say, echoing Lessing, 'I might have guessed' – as if he hadn't.

# References

Altered translations are indicated by an asterisk.

## 1 Rags to Riches

1  The quoted documents are preserved in Michael Pedersen Kierkegaard's papers in the Royal Library, Copenhagen.
2  Søren Kierkegaard, *Kierkegaard's Journals and Notebooks* [*KJN*], ed. Niels Jørgen Cappelørn, Alastair Hannay, David Kangas, Bruce H. Kirmmse, George Pattison, David Prossen, Joel D. Rasmussen, Vanessa Rumble and K. Brian Söderquist (Princeton, NJ, 2007–18) vol. II of XI, JJ:416.
3  *KJN* 2, JJ:198.
4  See Bruce H. Kirmmse, *Kierkegaard in Golden Age Denmark* (Bloomington and Indianapolis, IN, 1990), p. 260.
5  Cited ibid. p. 102.
6  *KJN* 3, Notebook 6:24 and *KJN* 5, NB10:153. This comment on fatherly love was made just after Kierkegaard finally completed his examinations on his only visit to Sædding. It was soon after that visit that Søren and his brother were confronted with their father's, to them, devastating confessions.
7  *KJN* 3, Notebook 6:29.
8  *KJN* 10, NB34.
9  Bruce H. Kirmmse, ed., *Encounters with Kierkegaard: A Life as Seen by His Contemporaries* [*EK*] (Princeton, NJ, 1996), p. 6.
10  *EK*, pp. 152–3, 175.
11  *EK*, pp. 196, 228.

## 2 The Bad Penny

1  Søren Kierkegaard, *S. Kierkegaard: Letters and Documents*, trans.
   H. Rosenmeier, *Kierkegaard's Writings* (KW), XXV (Princeton, NJ, 1978),
   pp. 4–5*. See also Bruce H. Kirmmse, ed., *Encounters with Kierkegaard:
   A Life as Seen by His Contemporaries* [EK] (Princeton, NJ, 1996), p. 17*.
2  Ibid., pp. 7 and 10.
3  Kierkegaard, *Letters and Documents*, pp. 4–5*; EK, p. 17*.
4  EK, pp. 8 and 9.
5  EK, p. 11.
6  EK, pp. 4–5, 7, 8, 10 and 11.
7  William Heinesen, *De Fortabte Spillemænd* [The Doomed Fiddlers]
   (Copenhagen, 1950), p. 144. My translation.
8  EK, p. 8.
9  Søren Kierkegaard, *Kierkegaard's Journals and Notebooks* [KJN], ed. Niels
   Jørgen Cappelørn, Alastair Hannay, David Kangas, Bruce H. Kirmmse,
   George Pattison, David Prossen, Joel D. Rasmussen, Vanessa Rumble
   and K. Brian Söderquist (Princeton, NJ, 2007–18), 2, JJ:352.
10  EK, p. 84.
11  Carl Weltzer, *Peter and Søren Kierkegaard* (Copenhagen, 1936), p. 25.
12  EK, p. 7.
13  EK, p. 3.
14  Søren Kierkegaard (Vigilius Haufniensis), *The Concept of Anxiety:
   A Simple Psychologically Oriented Deliberation in View of the Dogmatic
   Problem of Hereditary Sin*, trans. Alastair Hannay (New York, 2014),
   p. 51.
15  KJN 2, JJ:95.
16  KJN 5, NB8:36.
17  Søren Kierkegaard, *The Point of View*, trans. Howard V. Hong and Edna
   H. Hong (Princeton, NJ, 1998), p. 97.

## 3 Audience

1  Søren Kierkegaard, *Kierkegaard's Journals and Notebooks* [*KJN*], ed. Niels Jørgen Cappelørn, Alastair Hannay, David Kangas, Bruce H. Kirmmse, George Pattison, David Prossen, Joel D. Rasmussen, Vanessa Rumble and K. Brian Söderquist (Princeton, NJ, 2007–18), 11, Paper 9:6.

2  Søren Kierkegaard, *Upbuilding Discourses in Various Spirits*, trans. Howard V. Hong and Edna H. Hong (Princeton, NJ, 1993), p. 22.

3  *KJN* 1, AA:12, p. 16.

4  *KJN* 1, AA:13, italic removed.

5  *KJN* 1, AA:12, p. 19.

6  *KJN* 1, AA:12, p. 20*.

7  *KJN* 1, AA:12, pp. 21–2*.

8  *KJN* 1, AA:6, p. 10*.

9  *KJN* 1, AA:12, p. 16.

10  *KJN* 1, AA:12, p. 22.

11  *KJN* 1, AA:12, pp. 24–5.

12  *KJN* 1, AA:6, p. 9.

13  *KJN* 4, NB2:136.

14  *KJN* 9, NB30:93.

15  Bruce H. Kirmmse, ed., *Encounters with Kierkegaard: A Life as Seen by His Contemporaries* [*EK*] (Princeton, NJ, 1996), p. 63.

16  *EK*, p. 63.

17  *KJN* 11, Paper 254.

18  *EK*, p. 21.

19  *KJN* 1, AA:12, p. 24.

20  J. L. Heiberg, *On the Significance of Philosophy for the Present Age and Other Texts*, trans. Jon Stewart (Copenhagen, 2005), p. 117.

21  *KJN* 11, Paper 254.

22  Ibid.

23  Ibid.

24  *EK*, p. 22.

25  Lorenz Rerup, 'Fra litterær til politisk nasjonalisme', in Ole Feldbæk, *Dansk Identitetshistorie, 2: Et yndigt Land* (1789–1848) (Copenhagen, 1991), p. 359.

26  *EK*, pp. 22–3.

## 4 Faust and the Feminine

1 Søren Kierkegaard, *Prefaces: Light Reading for People in Various Estates According to Time and Opportunity*, trans. T. W. Nichol (Princeton, NJ, 2009), p. 44.

2 Søren Kierkegaard, *Kierkegaard's Journals and Notebooks* [*KJN*], ed. Niels Jørgen Cappelørn, Alastair Hannay, David Kangas, Bruce H. Kirmmse, George Pattison, David Prossen, Joel D. Rasmussen, Vanessa Rumble and K. Brian Söderquist (Princeton, NJ, 2007–18), 1, AA:15.

3 Josiah Thompson, *Kierkegaard* (New York, 1973), p. 44.

4 Bruce H. Kirmmse, ed., *Encounters with Kierkegaard: A Life as Seen by His Contemporaries* [*EK*] (Princeton, NJ, 1996), p. 207.

5 *KJN* 5, NB9:8.

6 *KJN* 11, Paper 97:1–6; 253; cf. *KJN* 3, Notebook 2:1,7, 10, 12–14.

7 See *KJN* 11, Paper 143 and *KJN* 2, DD:3.

8 *KJN* 7, NB10:116.

9 *KJN* 11, Paper 305:3.

10 *KJN* 11, Paper 591.

11 *KJN* 3, Notebook 2:12.

12 *KJN* 11, Paper 140.

13 *KJN* 3, Notebook 2:7.

14 *KJN* 11, Paper 35.

15 *KJN* 11, Paper 235:2.

16 *KJN* 11, Papers 142 and 145.

17 *KJN* 11, Paper 235:1.

18 *KJN* 3, Notebook 15:14.

19 *KJN* 1, AA:53.

20 In a letter from 23 February 1836. See H. F. Rørdam, *Peter Rørdam: Blade af hans Levnedsbog og Brevvexling fra 1806 til 1844* [Peter Rørdam: Pages from his Life History and Correspondence from 1806 to 1844], vol. I (Copenhagen, 1891), p. 78.

21 *KJN* 3, Notebook 15:4.

22 *KJN* 1, BB:44.

23 *KJN* 1, AA:54.

24 *KJN* 2, FF:54.

25 *KJN* 2, FF:43.

26  *KJN* 11, Paper 244. Nikolaus Lenau's *Faust: Ein Dicht* was published in 1836.

27  It has been suggested that the Gilleleje Testament and associated entries including the letter to his uncle in Brazil are part of an aborted Faustian project.

28  *EK*, p. 196.

29  *KJN* 6, NB13:86.

30  *KJN* 1, DD:96.

31  *EK*, p. 241.

32  *EK*, p. 12.

33  Søren Kierkegaard, *Early Polemical Writings*, trans. Julia Watkin (Princeton, NJ, 1990), p. 84.

34  *KJN* 1, DD:113 and 117.

35  *KJN* 1, DD:89.

36  *KJN* 1, DD:116.

37  *KJN* 1, DD:126.

38  *EK*, p. 229.

39  *KJN* 2, JJ:297.

40  *KJN* 4, NB4:152.

41  *KJN* 3, Notebook 5:19.

42  *EK*, p. 228.

43  *KJN* 2, EE:7.

44  *KJN* 3, Notebook 15:4.

45  *KJN* 1, BB:49.

46  *KJN* 6, NB12:138.

47  Walter Lowrie, *A Short Life of Kierkegaard* (Princeton, NJ, 2013), p. 17.

48  *KJN* 3, Notebook 6:31.

49  *KJN* 3, Notebook 6:24

50  *KJN* 3, Notebook 15:4.

51  Ibid.

52  Søren Kierkegaard, *S. Kierkegaard: Letters and Documents*, trans. H. Rosenmeier, KW XXV (Princeton, NJ, 1978), pp. 19–20.

53  *KJN* 3, Notebook 15:4.

54  *KJN* 6, NB12:138.

55  Kierkegaard, *Letters and Documents*, pp. 61–2.

56  *EK*, pp. 29–32, 199.

57  *Stages on Life's Way: Studies by Various Persons* (Princeton, NJ, 1988), p. 330.

58  *KJN* 3, Notebook 15:4.

59  *KJN* 3, Notebook 15:4 in margin.

60  KJN 3, Notebook 15:4*.

61  *EK*, pp. 162–3.

## 5  Either/Or

1  Søren Kierkegaard, *Kierkegaard's Journals and Notebooks* [*KJN*], ed. Niels Jørgen Cappelørn, Alastair Hannay, David Kangas, Bruce H. Kirmmse, George Pattison, David Prossen, Joel D. Rasmussen, Vanessa Rumble and K. Brian Söderquist (Princeton, NJ, 2007–18), 3, Notebook 15:4.

2  Ibid., 3, Notebook 8:2.

3  Ibid.

4  *KJN* 5, NB10:185.

5  *KJN* 5, NB10:192. See also Søren Kierkegaard, *Papers and Journals: A Selection*, trans. Alastair Hannay (London, 1996), pp. 562–3.

6  Ibid., p. 52.

7  *KJN* 9, NB28:54.

8  *Intelligensblade* (Copenhagen, 1843), pp. 285ff. See Joakim Garff, *Kierkegaard's Muse: The Mystery of Regine*, trans. Alastair Hannay (Princeton, NJ, 2017).

9  Søren Kierkegaard (Victor Eremita), *Either/Or: A Fragment of Life*, abridged edn, trans. Alastair Hannay (London, 1992), p. 589.

10  Ibid.

11  Søren Kierkegaard (Johannes *de silentio*), *Fear and Trembling: Dialectical Lyric*, trans. Alastair Hannay (London, 1985), p. 96.

12  G.W.F. Hegel, *Philosophy of Right*, trans. T. M. Knox (Oxford, 1971), p. 94.

13  Søren Kierkegaard, *Papers and Journals: A Selection*, trans. Alastair Hannay (London, 1996), p. 170.

14  Kierkegaard, *Either/Or*, p. 45.

15  Kierkegaard, *Papers and Journals: A Selection*, p. 165.

16  *KJN* 9, NB29:113.

17 See *KJN* 10 NB34:13: 'The sexual, this is the height of hum. egoism. Therefore, taken in a purely hum. way, not only the woman but also the man feels as though his life is lost, has failed, unless he gets married. Only the married are proper citizens in this world, the single pers. a stranger (which is indeed exactly what Xnty wants Xns to be – and what God wants the Xn to be in order to love him).' (Abbreviation in the original.)

18 Søren Kierkegaard, *S. Kierkegaard: Letters and Documents*, trans. H. Rosenmeier, KW XXV (Princeton, NJ, 1978), pp. 90, 105 and 136.

19 See *Søren Kierkegaards Skrifter K2–3* (Commentary vols II–III) (Copenhagen, 1997), p. 54.

20 Kierkegaard, *Papers and Journals: A Selection*, p. 170.

## 6 The Shower Bath

1 *Intelligensblade* (Copenhagen, 1843), 24, pp. 285ff. See Joakim Garff, *Kierkegaard's Muse: The Mystery of Regine*, trans. Alastair Hannay (Princeton, NJ, 2017).

2 Bruce H. Kirmmse, ed., *Encounters with Kierkegaard: A Life as Seen by His Contemporaries* [*EK*] (Princeton, NJ, 1996), p. 313.

3 Søren Kierkegaard, *S. Kierkegaard: Letters and Documents*, trans. H. Rosenmeier (Princeton, NJ, 1978), p. 154.

4 Søren Kierkegaard, *Kierkegaard's Journals and Notebooks* [*KJN*], ed. Niels Jørgen Cappelørn, Alastair Hannay, David Kangas, Bruce H. Kirmmse, George Pattison, David Prossen, Joel D. Rasmussen, Vanessa Rumble and K. Brian Söderquist (Princeton, NJ, 2007–18), 2, HH:8.

5 Ibid.

6 Ibid.

7 *KJN 2*, HH:12.

8 *KJN 6*, NB 12:147.

9 *Søren Kierkegaards Skrifter* (*SKS*) *K4* (commentary vol. IV), pp. 12ff.

10 Kierkegaard, *Letters and Documents*, p. 47.

11 Søren Kierkegaard, *Repetition and Philosophical Crumbs*, trans. M. G. Piety (Oxford, 2009), p. 37.

12 Ibid., p. 48.

13 Ibid., p. 76.

14  *KJN* 5, NB10:185.

15  Søren Kierkegaard, 'Two Upbuilding Discourses', in *Eighteen Upbuilding Discourses*, trans. Howard V. Hong and Edna H. Hong (Princeton, NJ, 1990).

16  *KJN* 8, NB25:109.

17  *KJN* 2, JJ:107.

18  Kierkegaard, Repetition, pp. 7 and 9 ('his beloved' changed to 'the beloved').

19  Ibid., p. 69.

20  Ibid., p. 81.

21  Ibid., p. 79.

22  *KJN* 3, JJ:116.

23  Garff, *Kierkegaard's Muse*, p. 73.

24  *KJN* 2, JJ:155.

25  Kierkegaard, *Repetition*, p. 74.

26  Kierkegaard, *Letters and Documents*, p. 154.

27  *KJN* 2, JJ:288.

28  *KJN* 2, JJ:167.

29  *SKS*, *K4*, p. 173. For a general account in Danish of the text's origins, see pp. 181–94.

30  Søren Kierkegaard (Vigilius Haufniensis), *The Concept of Anxiety: A Simple Psychologically Oriented Deliberation in View of the Dogmatic Problem of Hereditary Sin*, trans. Alastair Hannay (New York, 2014), pp. 145, 187.

31  Kierkegaard, *Repetition*, pp. 101–2.

32  Søren Kierkegaard (Victor Eremita), *Either/Or: A Fragment of Life*, abridged edn, trans. Alastair Hannay (London, 1992), p. 368.

33  See Garff, *Kierkegaard's Muse*, pp. 152 and 304 n. 9, and his reference to Jean Baudrillard, *De la séduction*, trans. Brian Singer (New York, 1990).

34  Søren Kierkegaard, *Prefaces: Light Reading for People in Various Estates According to Time and Opportunity*, trans. T. W. Nichol (Princeton, NJ, 2009), p. 10.

35  *KJN* 2, EE:136, p. 43.

36  See George Pattison, 'Kierkegaard and Copenhagen', in *The Oxford Handbook of Kierkegaard*, ed. John Lippitt and George Pattison (Oxford, 2013), p. 59.

37  *KJN* 7, NB30:41.

38  *KJN* 1, DD:31.

39  Søren Kierkegaard (Hilarius Bogbinder), *Stages on Life's Way: Studies by Various Persons* (Princeton, NJ, 1988), p. 14.

40  Ibid., p. 66.

41  Ibid., p. 175.

42  *KJN* 5, NB10:61.

43  *KJN* 2, JJ:115.

## 7  Winding Up

1  Søren Kierkegaard (Johannes Climacus), *Concluding Unscientific Postscript to the Philosophical Crumbs* [*Postscript*], trans. Alastair Hannay (Cambridge, 2009), p. 237.

2  Ibid., p. 437.

3  Ibid., p. 76.

4  Søren Kierkegaard, *Kierkegaard's Journals and Notebooks* [*KJN*], ed. Niels Jørgen Cappelørn, Alastair Hannay, David Kangas, Bruce H. Kirmmse, George Pattison, David Prossen, Joel D. Rasmussen, Vanessa Rumble and K. Brian Söderquist (Princeton, NJ, 2007–18), 2, JJ:414.

5  Kierkegaard, *Postscript*, p. 521.

6  Louis Mackey, *Kierkegaard: A Kind of Poet* (Philadelphia, PA, 1971), p. 192.

7  Kierkegaard, *Postscript*, pp. 3–4.

8  Ibid., p. 53.

9  Ibid., p. 60.

10  Ibid., p. 325.

11  Ibid., pp. 492 and 489.

12  Thomas à Kempis, *The Inner Life*, trans. Leo Sherley-Price (London, 2004), p. 95.

13  Kierkegaard, *Postscript*, p. 469.

14  Ibid., p. 521.

15  *KJN* 2, JJ:354.

16  *KJN* 4, NB:7

17  *KJN* 2, JJ:414, in the margin.

## 8 The Single Individual

1 See Elias Bredsdorff, *Corsaren, Goldschmidt og Kierkegaard* (Copenhagen, 1977).

2 Søren Kierkegaard, *Papers and Journals: A Selection*, trans. Alastair Hannay (London, 1996), p. 197.

3 *Søren Kierkegaards Skrifter* (*sks*) *k7*, pp. 74–5.

4 Søren Kierkegaard, *Kierkegaard's Journals and Notebooks* [*kjn*], ed. Niels Jørgen Cappelørn, Alastair Hannay, David Kangas, Bruce H. Kirmmse, George Pattison, David Prossen, Joel D. Rasmussen, Vanessa Rumble and K. Brian Söderquist (Princeton, nj, 2007–18), 4, nb:7.

5 There is a novel based on Møller's life by Henrik Strangerup: *The Seducer: It is Hard to Die in Dieppe*, trans. Sean Matin (London, 1990).

6 Bruce H. Kirmmse, ed., *Encounters with Kierkegaard: A Life as Seen by His Contemporaries* [*ek*] (Princeton, nj, 1996), p. 97.

7 *kjn* 4, nb:7.

8 Søren Kierkegaard, *A Literary Review*, trans. Alastair Hannay (London, 2001), pp. 84–5.

9 Ibid., p. 24.

10 Ibid., pp. 39, 55–6, 39 and 74–5.

11 Ibid., p. 80.

12 Ibid., intro. p. xx.

13 *kjn* 5, nb6:63.

14 *ek*, p. 117.

15 Kierkegaard, *A Literary Review*, p. 60.

16 Ibid., pp. 69, 87–92.

17 *ek*, pp. 65–7, 72–5.

18 *kjn* 4, nb:15 and 209.

19 Søren Kierkegaard (Johannes Climacus), *Concluding Unscientific Postscript to the Philosophical Crumbs* [*Postscript*], trans. Alastair Hannay (Cambridge, 2009), p. 157.

20 Ibid., p. 251.

21 *ek*, p. 237. See also p. 335, entry 26. Kirmmse takes *The Book on Adler* to be the work for whose preparation the right mood had been arranged.

22 Quoted in George Pattison, *Poor Paris*, Kierkegaard Studies Monograph (New York and Berlin, 1999), p. 111.

23 *kjn* 4, nb:107.

24  *KJN* 4, NB:114.

25  *KJN* 4, NB2:117. The earlier entry *KJN* 2, EE:105 is from 7 July 1839.

26  *KJN* 4, NB:123.

27  *KJN* 1, DD:32.

28  Søren Kierkegaard, *The Lily of the Field and the Bird of the Air*, trans. Bruce H. Kirmmse (Princeton, NJ, 2016), p. 77, translation slightly modified.

29  Ibid., pp. 78–9.

30  *KJN* 4, NB3:77.

31  Søren Kierkegaard, *The Point of View*, trans. Howard V. Hong and Edna H. Hong (Princeton, NJ, 1998), p. 118.

32  Ibid., p. 115.

33  *KJN* 5, NB10:68.

34  Kierkegaard, *The Point of View*, pp. 79 and 86; *KJN* 5, NB10:68.

35  *KJN* 6, NB11:204.

36  Søren Kierkegaard (Anti-Climacus), *The Sickness Unto Death: A Christian Psychological Exposition for Edification and Awakening*, trans. Alastair Hannay (London, 1989), p. 158.

37  *KJN* 6, NB13:37.

38  *KJN* 6, NB:204.

## 9  Thief and Martyr

1  Søren Kierkegaard, *Kierkegaard's Journals and Notebooks* [*KJN*], ed. Niels Jørgen Cappelørn, Alastair Hannay, David Kangas, Bruce H. Kirmmse, George Pattison, David Prossen, Joel D. Rasmussen, Vanessa Rumble and K. Brian Söderquist (Princeton, NJ, 2007–18), VI; NB12:118, 123, 150.

2  Bruce H. Kirmmse, ed., *Encounters with Kierkegaard: A Life as Seen by His Contemporaries* [*EK*] (Princeton, NJ, 1996), p. 37.

3  Ibid., p. 38.

4  *KJN* 5, NB7:10.

5  Søren Kierkegaard, *S. Kierkegaard: Letters and Documents*, trans. H. Rosenmeier, *Kierkegaard's Writings* (KW) XXV (Princeton, NJ, 1978), p. 329.

6  Søren Kierkegaard, *Practice in Christianity*, trans. Howard V. Hong and Edna Hong (Princeton, NJ, 1991), p. 7.

7   *KJN* 6 NB7:10.

8   *KJN* 5, NB6:74.

9   Søren Kierkegaard, *Without Authority*, trans. Howard V. Hong and Edna H. Hong (Princeton, NJ, 1997), pp. 106 and 235.

10  *KJN* 8, NB25:109.

11  Joakim Garff, *Kierkegaard's Muse: The Mystery of Regine*, trans. Alastair Hannay (Princeton, NJ, 2017), pp. 4–5.

12  *KJN* 8, NB22:146.

13  Ibid.

14  Ibid.

15  Ibid.

16  Garff, *Kierkegaard's Muse*, pp. 9–10.

17  *KJN* 3, Notebook 15:6.

18  The suggestion is made in Garff, *Kierkegaard's Muse*.

19  *EK*, p. 248.

20  Søren Kierkegaard, *The Moment and Late Writings*, trans. Howard V. Hong and Edna H. Hong (Princeton, NJ, 1998), pp. 5–6* (*Fædrelandet* [The Fatherland], February 1854).

21  *KW* XXIII, p. 21 (*Fædrelandet*, 26 January 1855).

22  *EK*, pp. 185–6.

23  See Bruce H. Kirmmse, *Kierkegaard in Golden Age Denmark* (Bloomington and Indianapolis, IN, 1990), p. 483, and Olaf Pedersen, *Lovers of Learning* (Copenhagen, 1993), pp. 206–8 and 256.

24  Kierkegaard, *The Moment and Late Writings*, pp. 157–8*.

25  NB19:77. The novelist (and film writer) who used P. L. Møller as a theme also wrote on how Peter Wilhelm Lund's excavations affected his beliefs in ways resembling Kierkegaard's experience. See Henrik Stangerup, *The Road to Lagoa Santa*, trans. B. Bluestone (London, 1988).

26  Kierkegaard, *The Moment and Late Writings*, p. 342.

27  *KJN* 4, NB3:77, p. 281.

## 10 Death and its Impact

1 Søren Kierkegaard, *Kierkegaard's Journals and Notebooks* [*KJN*], ed. Niels Jørgen Cappelørn, Alastair Hannay, David Kangas, Bruce H. Kirmmse, George Pattison, David Prossen, Joel D. Rasmussen, Vanessa Rumble and K. Brian Söderquist (Princeton, NJ, 2007–18), 11, Paper 591.

2 Bruce H. Kirmmse, ed., *Encounters with Kierkegaard: A Life as Seen by His Contemporaries* [*EK*] (Princeton, NJ, 1996), p. 248.

3 Søren Kierkegaard, *Papers and Journals: A Selection*, trans. Alastair Hannay (London, 1996), p. 653. Further references to this exchange can be found in pp. 649–56.

4 *EK*, p. 210.

5 *KJN* 9, NB29:95.

6 *KJN* 6, NB14:81 and 95.

7 Cf. *KJN* 6, NB14:108 and *KJN* 7, NB15:82.

8 *EK*, p. 136.

9 *EK*, p. 136.

10 *EK*, pp. 134–5.

11 *EK*, p. 135.

12 *Dansk Kirketidende* 1881, 22, repr. in Peter Christian Kierkegaards, *Samlede Skrifter* (Copenhagen, 1902–5), 4:127. See Bruce H. Kirmmse, '"Out With It": The Modern Breakthrough, Kierkegaard and Denmark', in *The Cambridge Companion to Kierkegaard*, ed. Alastair Hannay and Gordon D. Marino (Cambridge, 1998), pp. 36–7.

13 *EK*, p. 57.

## 11 In Time's Centrifuge

1 Steven Crites, 'The Author and the Authorship: Recent Kierkegaard Literature', *Journal of the American Academy of Religion*, vol. XXXVIII (March 1970), p. 38.

2 W. Kaufmann, ed., *From Dostoevsky to Sartre* (New York, 1956), p. 20.

3 See Søren Kierkegaard, *Kierkegaard's Journals and Notebooks* [*KJN*], ed. Niels Jørgen Cappelørn, Alastair Hannay, David Kangas, Bruce H. Kirmmse, George Pattison, David Prossen, Joel D. Rasmussen,

Vanessa Rumble and K. Brian Söderquist (Princeton, NJ, 2007–18), 7, NB17:45.

4 John Updike reviewing Joakim Garff, *Søren Kierkegaard: A Biography* (Princeton, NJ 2004) in the *New Yorker* (28 March 2005).

5 Will Rees, 'Cruel Intentions', *Times Literary Supplement* (29 September 2016).

6 *KJN* 4, NB3:22, from 1847.

7 *KJN* 6, NB11:204.

8 Søren Kierkegaard, *The Moment and Late Writings*, trans. Howard V. Hong and Edna H. Hong (Princeton, NJ, 1998), p. 324.

9 *KJN* 11, Paper 35.

10 *KJN* 9, NB36:19.

11 Søren Kierkegaard, *The Point of View*, trans. Howard V. Hong and Edna H. Hong (Princeton, NJ, 1998), p. 55.

12 Joakim Garff, *Søren Kierkegaard: A Biography*, trans. Bruce H. Kirmmse (Princeton, NJ, 2004), p. 556.

13 Ibid., p. 569.

14 *KJN* 5, NB9, 28:54.

15 Georg Brandes, *Søren Kierkegaard: En kritisk Fremstilling i Grundrids* [A Critical Exposition in Outline] (Copenhagen, 1877), p. 107.

16 Ibid. pp. 254–5. See also Julie K. Allen, 'Georg Brandes: Kierkegaard's Most Influential Mis-representative', in *Kierkegaard's Influence on Literature, Criticism, and Art, Tome II: Denmark*, ed. Jon Stewart (Farnham, 2013); Friedrich Nietzsche, *Selected Letters of Friedrich Nietzsche*, ed. Oscar Levy, trans. Anthony M. Ludovici, 1st edn (New York, 1921), p. 325.

17 Georg Lukács, *Soul and Form* (Cambridge, MA, 1971), p. 24; Georg Lukács, *Existentialisme ou Marxisme?* (Paris, 1948), p. 84.

18 Herbert Marcuse, *Reason and Revolution: Hegel and the Rise of Social Theory* (Boston, MA, 1960), p. 264.

19 Jean-Paul Sartre, 'The Singular Universal', trans. P. Goldberger, in *Kierkegaard: A Collection of Critical Essays*, ed. J. Thompson (New York, 1972), p. 231.

20 Ibid., p. 263.

21 Martin Heidegger, *Being and Time*, trans. Joan Stambaugh, rev. edn (Albany, NY, 2010), p. 225, fn 6.

22 Ibid., p. 184, fn 5.

23  Jürgen Habermas, 'Religion in the Public Sphere', *European Journal of Philosophy*, XIV/1 (2006), p. 17.

24  *KJN* 9, NB30:94.

25  Bruce H. Kirmmse, ed., *Encounters with Kierkegaard: A Life as Seen by His Contemporaries* [*EK*] (Princeton, NJ, 1996), pp. 193 and 217.

26  Ibid., p. 226.

27  *EK*, p. 65.

28  *EK*, p. 84.

29  *EK*, pp. 218 and 221.

30  *EK*, p. 177.

31  *EK*, pp. 45–6.

32  *EK*, p. 54; 'desk' altered to 'desks'.

# Bibliography

## Works by Kierkegaard

*Søren Kierkegaards Skrifter*, Bind. 1–28, Copenhagen: Søren Kierkegaard Forskningscenteret/Gads Forlag 1997–2011. A new critical edition of all of Kierkegaard's works, journals, notebooks, newspaper articles, and correspondence. (Available online: sks.dk)

## Published works

*Af en endnu Levendes Papirer* (1838)
*Om Begrebet Ironi med stadigt Hensyn til Socrat*es (1841)
*Enten/Eller. Et Livs-Fragment* (Victor Eremita) (1843)
*Gjentagelsen. Et Forsøg i den experimenterende Psychologi*
 (Constantin Constantius) (1843)
*Frygt og Bæven. Dialektisk Lyrik* (Johannes *de silentio*) (1843)
*To opbyggelige Taler* (1843)
*Tre opbyggelige Taler* (1843)
*Fire opbyggelige Taler* (1843*)*
*To opbyggleige Taler* (1844)
*Tre opbyggelige Taler* (1844)
*Philosophiske Smuler eller En Smule Philosophi* (Johannes Climacus) (1844)
*Begrebet Angest. En simpel psychologisk-paapegende Overveielse i Retning*
 *af det dogmatiske Problem om Arvesynden* (Vigilius Haufniensis) (1844)
*Forord. Morskabslæsning for enkelte Stænder efter Tid og Leilighed*
 (Nicolaus Notabene) (1844)
*Fire opbyggelige Taler* (1844)

*Tre Taler ved Tænkte Leiligheder* (1845)

*Stadier paa Livets Vei. Studier af Forskjellige* (Hilarius Bogbinder)
 (1845)

*Afsluttende uvidenskabelig Efterskrift til de philosophiske Smuler.*
 *Mimisk-pathetisk-dialektisk Sammenskrift, Existentielt Indlæg*
 (Johannes Climacus) (1846)

*En Literair Anmeldelse. To Tidsaldre, Novelle af Forfatteren til 'en*
 *Hverdagshistorie', udgiven af J. L. Heiberg* (1846)

*Opbyggelige Taler I forskjellig Aand* (1847)

*Kjerlighedens Gjerninger. Nogle christelige Overveielser i Talers Form*
 (1847)

*Christelige Taler* (1848)

*Lilien paa Marken og Fuglen under Himmelen. Tre gudelige Taler* (1849)

*Tvende ethisk-religieuse Smaa-Afhandlinger* (H. H.) (1849)

*Sygdommen til Døden. En christelig psychologisk Udvikling til Opbyggelse*
 *og Opvækkelse* (Anti-Climacus) (1849)

*'Ypperpræsten' – 'Tolderen' – 'Synderen'. Tre Taler ved Altergangen om*
 *Fredagen* (1849)

*Indøvelse i Christendom* (Anti-Climacus) (1850)

*En opbyggelig Tale* (1850)

*To Taler ved Altergangen om Fredagen* (1851)

*Om min Forfatter-Virksomhed* (1851)

*Til Selvprøvelse Samtiden anbefalet* (1851)

*Dette skal siges; saa være det da sagt* (1855)

*Hvad Christus dømmer om officiel Christendommen* (1855)

*Øieblikket* (1–9, 10 posthumously) (1855)


Posthumous (selected)


*Dømmer selv! Til selvprøvelse Samtiden anbefalet* (1851–2) (1856)

*Synspunktet for min Forfatter-Virksomhed. En ligefrem Meddelelse,*
 *Rapport til Historien* (1859)

## Works by Kierkegaard in English translation

*The Book on Adler: The Religious Confusion of the Present Age Illustrated by Magister Adler as a Phenomenon*, trans. Howard V. Hong and Edna H. Hong (Princeton, NJ, 2009)

*Christian Discourses/The Crisis and a Crisis in the Life of an Actress*, trans. Howard V. Hong and Edna H. Hong (Princeton, NJ, 2000)

*The Concept of Anxiety*, trans. Alastair Hannay (New York, 2014)

*The Concept of Irony with Continual Reference to Socrates/Notes of Schelling's Berlin Lectures*, trans. Howard V. Hong and Edna H. Hong (Princeton, NJ, 1992)

*Concluding Unscientific Postscript to the Philosophical Crumbs*, trans. Alastair Hannay (Cambridge, 2009)

*The Corsair Affair and Articles Related to the Writings*, trans. Howard V. Hong and Edna H. Hong (Princeton, NJ, 2009)

*Early Polemical Writings*, trans. Julia Watkin (Princeton, NJ, 1990)

*Eighteen Upbuilding Discourses*, trans Howard V. Hong and Edna H. Hong (Princeton, NJ, 1992)

*Either/Or: A Fragment of Life*, abridged and trans. Alastair Hannay (London, 1992)

*Fear and Trembling: Dialectical Lyric*, trans. Alastair Hannay (London, 1985)

*For Self-examination and Judge for Yourself*, trans. Howard V. Hong and Edna H. Hong (Princeton, NJ, 1991)

*Letters and Documents*, trans. H. Rosenmeier (Princeton, NJ, 2009)

*The Lily of the Field and the Bird of the Air: Three Godly Discourses*, trans. Bruce H. Kirmmse (Princeton, NJ, 2016)

*A Literary Review*, trans. Alastair Hannay (London, 2001)

*The Moment and Late Writings*, trans. Howard V. Hong and Edna H. Hong (Princeton, NJ, 2009)

*The Point of View*, trans. Howard V. Hong and Edna H. Hong (Princeton, NJ, 1998)

*Practice in Christianity*, trans. Howard V. Hong and Edna H. Hong (Princeton, NJ, 1991)

*Prefaces*, trans. T. W. Nichol (Princeton, NJ, 2009)

*Purity of Heart is to Will One Thing*, trans. Douglas Steere (New York, 1956)

*Repetition and Philosophical Crumbs*, trans M. G. Piety (Oxford, 2009)

*The Sickness Unto Death*, trans. Alastair Hannay (London, 1989)
*Stages on Life's Way: Studies by Various Persons*, trans. Howard V. Hong
and Edna H. Hong (Princeton, NJ, 1988)
*Three Discourses on Imagined Occasions*, trans. Howard V. Hong and Edna
H. Hong (Princeton, NJ, 1992)
*Upbuilding Discourses in Various Spirits*, trans. Howard V. Hong and Edna
H. Hong (Princeton, NJ, 1993, 2009)
*Works of Love*, trans. Howard V. Hong and Edna H. Hong (Princeton, NJ, 1998)

## Journals and Notebooks

*Kierkegaard's Journals and Notebooks,* ed. Niels Jørgen Cappelørn, Alastair
Hannay, David Kangas, Bruce H. Kirmmse, George Pattison, David
Prossen, Joel D. Rasmussen, Vanessa Rumble and K. Brian Söderquist,
vols I–XI (Princeton, NJ, 2007–18)
*Papers and Journals: A Selection*, trans. Alastair Hannay (London, 1996)

## On Kierkegaard

The present work draws on the author's *Kierkegaard: A Biography* and on
several other works listed below but, in particular, Bruce H. Kirmmse's
*Encounters with Kierkegaard* (trans. Bruce H. Kirmmse and Virginia
R. Laursen of Kirmmse, ed., *Søren Kierkegaard Truffet. Et liv set af hans
samtidige*) (Copenhagen, 1996) and Joakim Garff's *Kierkegaard's Muse:
The Riddle of Regine*, trans. Alastair Hannay (Princeton, NJ, 2017).

Davenport, John J., and Anthony Rudd, eds, *Kierkegaard after MacIntyre:
Essays on Freedom, Narrative and Virtue* (Chicago, IL, 2001)
Evans, C. Stephen, *Kierkegaard: An Introduction* (Cambridge, 2009)
Garff, Joakim, *Søren Kierkegaard: A Biography*, trans. Bruce H. Kirmmse
(Princeton, NJ, 2004)
—, *Kierkegaard's Muse: The Riddle of Regine*, trans. Alastair Hannay
(Princeton, NJ, 2017)
Hannay, Alastair, *Kierkegaard: A Biography* (Cambridge, 2001)
—, *Kierkegaard and Philosophy: Selected Essays* (London, 2003)

Hannay, Alastair, and Gordon D. Marino, eds, *The Cambridge Companion to Kierkegaard* (Cambridge, 1998)

Kirmmse, Bruce H., *Encounters with Kierkegaard: A Life as Seen by His Contemporaries* (Princeton, NJ, 1996)

—, *Kierkegaard in Golden Age Denmark* (Bloomington and Indianapolis, IN, 1990)

Lippit, John, and George Pattison, eds, *The Oxford Handbook of Kierkegaard* (Oxford, 2013)

Lowrie, Walter, *A Short Life of Kierkegaard* (Princeton, NJ, 2013)

Mackey, Louis, *Kierkegaard: A Kind of Poet* (Philadelphia, PA, 1971)

Marino, Gordon D., ed., *The Quotable Kierkegaard* (Princeton, NJ, 2016)

Mooney, Edward F., *Excursions with Kierkegaard* (London, 2013)

—, ed., *Ethics, Love and Faith in Kierkegaard: Philosophical Engagements* (Bloomington and Indianapolis, IN, 2008)

Rée, Jonathan, and Jane Chamberlain, *Kierkegaard: A Critical Reader* (Oxford, 1998)

Stewart, Jon, ed., *A Companion to Kierkegaard* (Malden, MA, and Oxford, 2015)

Stokes, Patrick, *The Naked Self: Kierkegaard and Personal Identity* (Oxford, 2015)

Scholarly debate can be found and traced in the *International Kierkegaard Commentary*, ed. Robert L. Perkins (Macon, Georgia, and essays with reports on recent work in *Kierkegaard Studies* (*Yearbook* and *Monograph Series*), ed. the Kierkegaard Research Center in Copenhagen (Berlin and New York); and the 'Kierkegaard Newsletter' from St Olaf College, Northfield, Minnesota, which houses the Hong Kierkegaard Library (available at wp.stolaf.edu).

# Acknowledgements

I take this opportunity to express my gratitude to all those colleagues whose writings and conversations through many years have contributed to my appreciation of a thinker whose name I first chanced on in 1957. That was in a lecture series on modern philosophy at Edinburgh when Kierkegaard was associated in Britain with literature and religion. It was not until being asked by the editor to contribute a work on Kierkegaard in his 'Arguments of the Philosophers' series that I returned to Kierkegaard. I suspect the request was due to a chance remark in that editor's company about having found Kierkegaard interesting. This thin basis gained strength through yet another stroke of luck: to finance the completion of my doctoral dissertation on quite another topic I had been offered by a temporary copy editor's job with a Norwegian publisher. Finding Ibsen's Norwegian and Kierkegaard's Danish to be almost identical, I was able before long to read Kierkegaard profitably in the original. My thanks are therefore also due to the memory of Peter Frøstrup, the friend who got me that job, to the editor, my good colleague Ted Honderich, and not least to Dame Fortune.

More immediately, I thank my editor at Reaktion, Amy Salter, for her friendly and effective steering of the text on its way to the press, Susannah Jayes for her indispensable advice and management of the illustrations, and an unnamed but persistent copy-editor for eliciting as well as offering improvements in wording and style.

# Photo Acknowledgements

The author and the publishers wish to express their thanks to the below sources of illustrative material and /or permission to reproduce it.

The City Museum, Copenhagen: pp. 20, 69; The Museum of National History, Frederiksborg: pp. 15, 27, 49, 59, 100; Øregaard Museum, Hellerup: p. 52; The Royal Library, Denmark: pp. 10, 21, 40, 44, 45, 61, 73, 74, 86, 123, 125, 126, 134, 147, 148, 171, 180.